Agile Management

Ángel Medinilla

Agile Management

Leadership in an Agile Environment

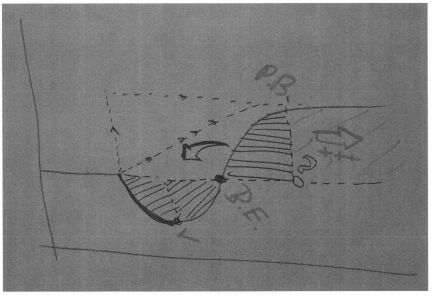

"The J-Curve" – hand drawing by the author at an Agile seminar

 Springer

Ángel Medinilla
Proyectalis
Mairena del Aljarafe, Seville
Spain

ISBN 978-3-642-28908-8   ISBN 978-3-642-28909-5 (eBook)
DOI 10.1007/978-3-642-28909-5
Springer Heidelberg New York Dordrecht London

Library of Congress Control Number: 2012944561

ACM Computing Classification (1998): K.6, K.7, D.2

Printed on acid-free paper

Springer is part of Springer Science+Business Media (www.springer.com)

Preface

This book is based on my own experience while working with companies as an external Agile consultant. I have been helping all kinds of companies, from 12 to 500 employees, to successfully implement Agile frameworks, and I have trained several thousands of managers and developers on topics like Scrum, Kanban, Agile management, team coaching or change management. Client profiles include telco, banking, videogames, software factories, mobile applications, government, logistics, retail, dot-coms, on-line services, start-ups or media companies. Although I have met really skeptical people, I have never been at a place where I thought 'It's impossible to be Agile here'. That is why I ask you to be open-minded through the reading of this book: remember that the mind is like a parachute; it only works when it is open.

Nevertheless, most of my Agile 'book of tricks' is based on other people's research, books, blogs and other forms of work that I have studied and used myself. I have tried to give credit to all of them, although this may not be always possible, as sometimes I cannot distinguish between my own ideas and the ones I am borrowing from somebody else. Innovation, I believe, is achieved by constant re-combination of ideas, so I just hope I introduce some new approaches to the field of Agile management by combining the several sources I usually integrate on my daily practice. If all I end up with is a list of interesting resources, I really hope I can save you some time and guide you to the useful ones.

This book is aimed at Agile managers, team leaders, change agents, evangelists and anyone trying to push Agile further in his or her organization. Enterprise agility and general resistance to change, both by management and the organization as a whole, are recurrent memes in the Agile community, and I hope to trigger interesting conversations on how to move Agile out of the team's environment and to the whole system, thus building better companies to work in.

As this is a book about Agile from a management perspective, it has a strong bias to software development – remember that the word Agile comes from the Manifesto for Agile *Software* Development. Anyway, the methods described are suitable and useful for any company that relies on the talent of their employees and operates on a complex and changing environment. But this is not a book about Agile or Lean. I will dedicate a whole chapter to introduce some basics about these frameworks and recommend a comprehensive list of great resources for readers who want to learn about them. Again, you do not need to be a Lean or Agile expert – or even want to implement Agile at your organization to obtain some benefit from the many ideas proposed in this book.

Management is a fuzzy area. I have tried to be as practical as possible and propose actual things you can try at your workplace, but of course a 5-person start-up will not need the same tools or practices as a Fortune 500. It is up to you to decide how to use the numerous principles enlisted in this book to better suit your environment.

Overall, if you want to change the way you manage, you have to change your paradigm set of what management is about. From an Agile perspective, we have learned that management is not about deciding on your own, telling people what to do and then supervising and controlling them until they achieve the desired results. We live in a different world from the one that most of the management experts of the twentieth century experienced, and companies that strive for success and excellence will need a new kind of managers.

Agile Managers

Acknowledgments

To all of you, readers (and specially buyers :-) of this book. Not only are you making this book possible, but you are also showing your commitment to change the world to a better place, starting with the place you are probably spending most of our life: your workplace.

Thanks to Ralf Gerstner, from Springer, who contacted me after my Agile Management tutorial at XP2011 and believed that it would make good content for a book. You would not have this in your hands if it weren't for his trust.

To all the good managers I have met in my life who taught me how joyful work can be when you feel part of something great. You took a stand and demonstrated that management is not a zero-sum game of survival, power harvesting and blame avoiding. While other managers were making their employees' lives miserable, calling them "resources" and treating them as mindless drones, subordinates, inferiors, commodities or expendable materials, you considered them colleagues in the challenge of succeeding. Now I know that this was not something natural, but the consequence of years and years of constant fight against a cruel juggernaut called The System. For me, that's what life's about.

To a whole bunch of Agile writers, many of whom I have met over the years, who have taught me so much about how things can be more natural, stress-less, efficient and fun. Special thanks to Mary and Tom Poppendieck, Mike Cohn, Henrik Kniberg, Lyssa Adkins, Jurgen Appelo, Jeff Sutherland, Ken Schwaber and Jeff Patton.

To my clients, specially those who trusted me when I started and no one knew what this Agile thing was about. Special thanks to all the development teams I have been coaching since I started my Agile career. You rock!

To my Aikido Senseis at Kisei Dojo, Antonio and Marcos Peña, for bringing balance to my life. *Domo Arigato Gozaimashita.*

To my wife, who has made my life so full of joy and love that it almost hurts (and I love the way it does).

To my son who, at the age of five, learned that there is nothing impossible, maybe just very difficult, and constantly reminds me about it.

Contents

Part I

The Agile Manager

A Brief History of Management

From Silver Back Gorillas to Konosuke Matsushita

1

Leaders and Managers

One of the main problems I have found when talking to people about Agile management is that not everyone used the same meaning for the concept of "manager" or "leader." In fact, I seldom find two people who use these words with the same meaning. And of course, that is what I call the "three blind men and the elephant" situation.

You probably know the story already: three blind monks were guided to an elephant so they could admire this mighty animal, and each of them touched a different part. "The elephant is like a pillar," said the first one, hugging a leg. "No it's not," replied the second one, "it's more like a snake." Of course, he was holding the trunk. Then the third one said "you fools, an elephant is like a manta ray," while touching the elephant's ear.

All of them were wrong. But all of them were partially right.

Think of this story because you are probably already experiencing something similar in many meetings. People quarrel about the "strategy" or the "teams" or the "projects," and we assume that everyone understands the same thing when we use these words. Why don't you try this in your next meeting? When you find yourselves stuck on a topic, ask everyone to write on a piece of paper what's the question you are trying to answer right now. The results may surprise you. If someone says "but there is no actual question," then why on earth are you discussing. You are just wasting your time; go on to the next topic.

For the sake of this book, I will refer to "leaders" as role models. Someone you want to follow and who inspires you with his or her actions.

Á. Medinilla, *Agile Management*, DOI 10.1007/978-3-642-28909-5_1,
© Springer-Verlag Berlin Heidelberg 2012

The image I want to picture is that of Gandhi, Martin Luther King, Nelson Mandela, John Lennon, or Lady Gaga.

> "A leader is best when people barely know he exists, when his work is done, his aim fulfilled, they will say: we did it ourselves."
>
> –Lao Tzu

There are different types of leaders. Probably, in your workplace, you have someone who is the technical leader. He is the alpha geek, the one everyone looks at when you have to take a risky technical decision and the one whose help is always needed when trying to fix some architectural problem.

You can also have a cultural leader, someone who embodies what being a part of this company means, someone whose behavior people mimic. And then there are thought leaders, negotiation leaders, strategy leaders, product leaders... Even a party leader! Close your eyes, think for a second... Ah, there he is, you already know who the party leader in your workplace is, don't you?

And Agile leaders. This is one of the things this book is about.

On the other hand, the meaning I'll use for "manager" is someone responsible and accountable to some degree for organizing things in a way that makes everything work as desired. He will be responsible for corporate goals, so he will give some sort of directives to others with the aim of coordinating and aligning efforts, and sometimes he will set boundaries and constraints to others. The manager is someone who thinks he is in control of something. Of course, as you will learn through this book, this last assumption is probably wrong.

> *"Oogway*: My friend, the panda will never fulfill his destiny, nor you yours until you let go of the illusion of control.
> *Shifu*: Illusion?
> *Oogway*: Yes.
> [points at peach tree]
> *Oogway*: Look at this tree, Shifu: I cannot make it blossom when it suits me nor make it bear fruit before its time.

> *Shifu*: But there are things we *can* control: I can control when the fruit will fall, I can control where to plant the seed: that is no illusion, Master!
> *Oogway*: Ah, yes. But no matter what you do, that seed will grow to be a peach tree. You may wish for an apple or an orange, but you will get a peach."
>
> —Kung Fu Panda (Dreamworks, 2008)

Because of my background, I tend to divide managers into two main types: project managers and line managers. Project managers will take care of actual work, while line managers will work on the system, the environment, and the business model. Project managers will set schedules, delivery dates, budgets, and priorities, while line managers will decide the company strategy, define business processes, set marketing goals, coordinate efforts of different departments, or define the product roadmap.

Some managers will be a mixed type. They will care for both the projects and the processes. They will hire people, divide them into teams, assign work to each team and also define the budget for the next year, approve internal processes, deal with other departments, report to management meetings, and define their own department's strategy, goals, and needs.

Usually, they will do more of one part than the other. Some of these managers will tend to work more at the team level, micromanaging every single action and not defending them from company politics, while others will focus on the company's side in search of personal status and forget about their own people's needs. Theoretically, it is possible to do both things right. But, only in theory, theory and reality are the same thing.

In reality, they are not.

A leader does not need to be a manager, and the reverse is also true. All managerial literature seems to accept the dogma that managers must become leaders to reach their full potential. Well, in fact it really helps. But think about a warehouse manager. Maybe he is working on his own, or maybe the warehouse crew was replaced long ago by automated material handling systems. But he is still the manager. He is expected to improve the system, maintain the service level, report the warehouse status when needed, and deal with warehouse clients and suppliers. And he does not need to be a "leader" to be a superb warehouse manager. Even if he is managing a crew of 20 workers, he does not need to be the leader of this crew. Maybe Bob, the warehouse worker, is the crew's leader, and he acts as an interface with the manager, while the manager acts as an interface for the warehouse with the rest of the company.

In fact, a company I worked for had a funny de-motivational poster hanging on a wall that read something like "Leaders are like eagles: we have neither of them here."[1] And boy, did they have managers... Please understand I'm not making the case for leaderless management; just trying to define the difference between both concepts and proving that you can have one without the other, although having both of them is of course the preferable state for the Agile manager.

So now that we've set a simple definition of leader and manager, let's see where leadership came from and how it slowly transformed into what we call today management.

> "So much of what we call management consists in making it difficult for people to work."
>
> –Peter Drucker

Leadership Among Apes

Let me state that I'm not a qualified primatologist. Probably neither are you but, still, I think we've both probably seen enough National Geographic Society documentaries as to easily answer this question: do apes have leaders? What is their role? How do they choose a leader?

Apes are not good survivors on their own. They don't have sharp claws, they don't run too fast, and their only hope of survival in the open field is to try to look as less desirable a meal as possible to a potential predator (think of a baboon's back while he flees from a predator: if I was that predator, I would think twice about eating *that*). That is why most of them, especially the smaller ones, tried to live up in the trees, where only the most agile felines can hunt them.

---

[1] You can find more de-motivational quotes at http://www.despair.com/. They will give you some clues on motivational anti-patterns (see Chap. 4).

But, somehow, some of them found out something that changed their world.

If they gathered together to form a tribe, they were powerful. Few predators will dare to attack a whole tribe of screaming, chest-banging, stick-waving apes. So tribes survived and lone riders became extinct. That is the same reason why we, human beings, are all tribal. Human tribes were able to defend themselves and hunt bigger preys, while solo hunters starved or were attacked by saber-toothed tigers.

When the tribes were formed, conflicts aroused. Apes fought for status, food, access to females, and even the best branches in the tree. Some form of mediation was needed for the tribe to survive, and that is where the alpha males came in handy.

Alpha males are not necessarily the strongest, oldest, or biggest apes in the community but rather the most political individuals, the ones who can form enough alliances that will provide support for them.

In fact, if a stronger individual from the outside is fool enough to come into the tribe and try to challenge the dominant male, the whole tribe will probably beat him up and kick him out.

So the leader is the one who gets the most followers. This is something crucial to understand leadership and management in our age. Leadership, from an evolutionary perspective, is not *imposed* but *accepted*. You can't just appoint someone as "leader" and expect everyone to follow him.

> "*Chief Wanadi*: If I tell a man to do what he does not want to do, I am no longer chief."
> –The Emerald Forest (Christel Films & Embassy Pictures Corporation, 1985)

Once a leader is accepted by a group of apes, what is his role? Well, in fact, he doesn't do much most of the time. He sits around while females groom him and bring him food. Other males show him respect by making submissive gestures. And that seems to be all until some conflict arises: then the dominant male will immediately take part and intimidate the fighting apes to end the dispute. Of course, he is also expected to be in the front line when a leopard shows up. In fact, recent studies show that the stress level of the alpha male is much bigger than the one on the betas.[2] Sorry alpha males, it comes with the job.

That's it: the main role of the leader in a community of apes is to defend it and, what is more important, keep the community united.

Some people may think that this is only relevant to apes but has nothing in common with the complex politics of human organizations. Think twice. Studies show that most humans have been socially, psychologically, and biologically hardwired with the need for a single dominant male figure to rule their communal lives. Almost all anthropoid primate societies are managed in a very similar way. This could partially explain why, still in the twenty-first century, women find it difficult to prosper in management careers: their primitive male colleagues are releasing their inner ape (sorry ladies, but please don't kill the messenger).

For instance, in his book *King of the Mountain*, Arnold Ludwig states that political leaders are almost universally males. They also tend to have greater access to sexual partners (for the joy of tabloids) and have larger number of children. He also explains that there are no special skills or abilities necessary for being a leader, although demonstration of physical bravery and aggressive behavior helps to achieve and maintain the leader's position. The description of this behavior will very probably bring you memories of some of the bosses you've met in the past.

Want more evidence of the presence of the inner ape in our business organizations? Leadership qualities are unconsciously ascribed to taller people because our inner ape thinks that they will be more capable of protecting the tribe. Multiple studies show that tall and handsome men make more charismatic leaders. These studies prove that education, grades, and experience play a significant role, but they are not as important as individual qualities such as charisma, magnetism, reputation, and tact.

For instance, Timothy Judge and Daniel Cable, from the University of Florida, analyzed data from 8,500 participants from adolescence to adulthood, and found out that there is an implicit bias toward taller people in terms of promotions and salaries.[3] That's it: tall people make more money. And they have more chances of becoming the president of the United States, granted that out of

---

[2] Gesquiere LR, Learn NH, Carolina M, Simao M, Onyango PO, Alberts SC, Altmann J (2011) Life at the top: rank and stress in wild male baboons. Science 333(6040):357–360.

[3] Judge TA, Cable DM (2004) The effect of physical height on workplace success and income: preliminary test of a theoretical model. J Appl Psychol 89(3):428–441.

forty-three American presidents, only five have been a bit below average height, and most of them have been several inches above the norm for their times.[4]

The only difference between ape tribes and our modern-times organizations is that leadership, in the latter, is *imposed* instead of *accepted*. Maybe you choose to work for a particular manager because you decide to *follow* him, but many times you don't even know your boss before your first day at work, or have as little as a couple of hours out of a stressful job interview to form for yourself an opinion of who is the person you are going to spend several years working for. And then, of course, the company can change this manager without your consent.

Feudalism, Empires, and the Origin of Hierarchies

Even before the birth of the first human civilizations, apes already had some forms of hierarchies in their communities. Individuals, both males and females, have distinct status in the tribe depending on the influence on others, and individuals other than the alpha male can influence and even dominate individuals of lower rank.

Curiously enough, not only was this hardwiring toward hierarchy inherited by humans but also the higher stress levels and the higher probability of suffering from cardiovascular and depression/anxiety-like syndromes by people in higher hierarchical positions. Yes, there is a study on that.[5]

It is no surprise then that, when human tribes grew and the same individual ruled many human tribes, the hierarchy was instantly and instinctively established. And this led later to the emergence of feudalism as a system.

Although feudalism is a term often used to refer to the social system in medieval Europe, it can in fact be used to define many other political systems, including the Shoguns in Japan or the Pharaohs in ancient Egypt. In feudalism you have a common leader, the king, but he is not able to rule the country on his own, so he relies on nobles and warlords who take an oath of loyalty to the king. This way, although warlords had a fair freedom of acts on their lands, they could unite together under the flag of the king to defend the country against foreign enemies.

---

[4] Sommers PM (2002) Is presidential greatness related to height?. College Math J 33(1):14–16.

[5] Zink C, Meyer-Lindenberg A et al (2008) Know your place: neural processing of social hierarchy in humans. Neuron 58(2):273–283.

So, in modern terms, feudalism was a sort of scalability solution for the tribal system. Vassals were loyal to the king first, and then to their feudal lord.

Lords were able to rule the lives of their vassals and peasants almost unlimitedly (think on *droit de seigneur*), and they in exchange trusted the lord to protect them against foreign enemies, mediate on disputes, and make them prosper. Of course, there was a core element of fear that helped the system work, both fear of external threats and the military forces and the almost unlimited power of the feudal lord.

A more centralized solution was the empire. In this case, an army was needed, many times in the form of permanent occupation forces (fixed garrisons). When empires fell and were decentralized, they reverted to the state of feudal system, both with the presence of a king or just as a conglomerate of fiefs ruled by warlords.

I believe that there is a big similarity between the primitive social structures and the way that modern companies are ruled. Kings (CEOs) can't control the whole company on their own, so they rely on nobles (managers) to actually take control of smaller bits of the empire. These fiefs (departments) are populated by vassals (workers) who are hired by the manager, but must be loyal to the country (company) and the king. I mean, the CEO. Managers are able to rule the lives of their workers with unlimited power, and the workers submit to the manager's will in the hope that he will protect them against enemies, mediate on disputes, and make them prosper. There is also a "fear of the manager" component because he can decide about your life (promotion) or death (you are fired).

> "There's something fundamental about organizations and leadership that makes it almost impossible for people inside a business to change their own industry: Industries are based on formats that are basically legacies of military hierarchies."
>
> –Ricardo Semler

In fact, there is an interesting difference. Feudal warlords would never address a vassal and say "hey Bob, I have seen your last crop, good job, but... Do you think you could grow the corn again *but with half the space between rows*? I need them on my granary on June... Keep up the good job!"

That's it: they had an arrangement with vassals with boundaries, constraints, and goals on how the land was granted and what payment was expected for the use of the land, but the actual work was entrusted to them. A lord would never micromanage his vassals.

So here is some advice for the twenty-first-century managers: don't try to read those management books about Machiavelli, Sun Tzu, or the Laws of Power. You are not an Italian prince, nor a Japanese Shogun, nor a *gangsta* rapper. We expect different things from you.

We expect you to be an Agile manager.

Taylorism and Fordism

Business models saw few improvements from the birth of the first civilizations until the industrial age. Probably the more remarkable events were the emergence of trading companies and the rise of the *bourgeoisie*.

For centuries, production methods remained more or less the same: craftsmen determined the way to produce things, often taking decisions by tradition, rules of thumb, and personal skills. Craftsmen maybe took a couple of apprentices, and there was a cap to the quantity of items a workshop could actually deliver. Even at the beginning of the industrial age, most of the machines, including cars and motorbikes, were produced by craftsmen following an artisanal process.

This lasted until the beginning of the twentieth century, when the ideas of an American mechanical engineer named Frederick Winslow Taylor created an industrial revolution. His theory of scientific management allowed unprecedented production capacity by synthesizing workflows: this means that the production process was studied, documented, and standardized, and every worker was trained to do only a small and specific part of the production workflow in the way that the engineer believed was the best.

Taylor addressed issues as efficiency, waste, and work ethics. But the underlying principle in his theory was that workers were lazy, and didn't know the best way to do things and intense managerial control was needed to obtain the desired results. He also believed in an incentive system that rewarded productivity and punished those who deviated from the standard way of doing things. The paradigm was to take ideas out of the heads of the managers and into the hands of the workers.

Henry Ford was possibly one of the best-known examples of the application of Taylor's model. The development of the assembly line allowed mass production of the Ford-T, which lowered its unit price and revolutionized the world.

> "Why is it each time I ask for a pair of hands, they come attached to a brain?"
>
> –Henry Ford

Taylorism (and, later on, Fordism) led to a deep differentiation of blue-collar and white-collar classes at the workplace, as well as other severe side effects: labor-versus-capital fight, strikes, unionism, micromanagement, de-motivation in the workplace, and de-humanitization of the workforce (as depicted in Charles Chaplin's movie *Modern Times*). But who cared about the motivation of workers when you could find new ones for a dime a dozen and train them for a lifetime in three hours?

In later stages, Taylorism even caused the erosion of employment in developed economies via both offshoring and automation. Taylor was also one of the first management consultants, if you want to blame him for something more.

The Machine That Changed the World

This changed in the second half of the twentieth century, mainly by the influence of two sources: the rise of the Japanese methods of production (Lean manufacturing) and the appearance of workers of a new kind: knowledge workers.

During the 1980s, the almighty American car industry started to worry about what was going on in Japan. They were making more cars, faster and cheaper. They needed half the factory space, half the time, half the labor, and virtually no stock or inventory. Even more frightening, the quality of the cars was outstanding!

So American engineers and scientists started looking at the Japanese production methods, and what they found out there changed the face of the world. In fact, three of the most well-known researchers of the Japanese production methods were James P. Womack, Daniel T. Jones, and Daniel

Roos, who published their findings in a 1991 book they titled *The Machine that Changed the World*.

Although Japanese engineers assured that their main inspiration were Taylor and Ford, the differences with the way things were done in America were huge. The first thing that the Americans noticed was that the whole Japanese system was conceived around the idea of increasing the delivery of value to the client by reducing or eliminating any kind of materials or activities that didn't contribute directly to this delivery of value. These unnecessary activities, which Japanese engineers labeled as *waste*, were categorized, studied, and systematically attacked by a process of continuous improvement or *Kaizen*. A whole bunch of methods, practices, and tools were imported to the western industries, thus actually changing the way everyone worked. Today, virtually all world-class manufacturers use terms as just-in-time production, pull approach, flow, system thinking, standardized work, waste reduction, or built-in quality. All of them came from the study of Japanese production methods, especially those developed at Toyota Motor Corporation, whose Toyota Production System (TPS) was the main subject for the studies on the new way of running manufacturing plants.

But the differences were not only in the processes. The human factor was at the core of the Japanese methods, which had been named "Lean production" by the American researchers. Japanese managers talked about things like pride of the workforce, ownership of the system, empowerment, mastery, excellence, motivation, and, yes, leadership.

In fact, many Lean consultants will tell you that western companies adopting Japanese production methods, processes, and tools very frequently can't reach the Japanese performance and quality, because their implementations are focused on those tools, but their management style remains the same.

"We are going to win and the industrial west is going to lose. There is nothing much you can do about it, because the reasons for your failure are within yourselves. Your firms are built on the Taylor model; with your bosses doing the thinking while the workers wield the screwdrivers, you're convinced deep down that this is the right way to run a business. For you, the essence of management is getting the ideas out of the heads of the bosses into the hands of labor.

We are beyond the Taylor model. Business, we know, is now so complex and difficult, the survival of firms so hazardous in an environment increasingly unpredictable, competitive and fraught with danger, that their continued existence depends on the day-to-day mobilization of every ounce of intelligence. For us, the core of

(continued)

management is precisely this art of mobilizing and pulling together the intellectual resources of all employees in the service of the firm. Because we have measured better than you the scope of the new technological and economic challenges, we know that the intelligence of a handful of technocrats, however brilliant and smart they may be, is no longer enough to take them up with a real chance of success. Only by drawing on the combined brainpower of all its employees can a firm face up to the turbulence and constraints of today's environment."

–Konosuke Matsushita[6]

The Rise of a New Species: Knowledge Workers

As stated previously, the second source of change of the management model during the second half of the twentieth century was the rise of a new species: knowledge workers.

The term is often credited to Peter F. Drucker, who used it in his 1959 book *Landmarks of Tomorrow*. In it, Drucker talked about a new kind of worker who did not perform manual tasks but used his knowledge to analyze problems, develop products, or design solutions. This included engineers, architects, lawyers, designers, software developers, and a whole breed of new "white-collar" workers.

He also wrote that the management's new role in today's organization is to make knowledge more productive. Central to his philosophy was the belief that highly skilled people are an organization's most valuable resource, and that a manager's job is to prepare and free people to perform.

The rise of the knowledge worker brought new challenges: there was no easy and perfect way to define their duty and reduce it to a set of repetitive tasks to perform, and their productivity was not easy to measure. The paradigm of the pieces-per-hour productivity was not valid anymore, and managers realized that, in a knowledge environment, the best performing workers in the world could be 20, 50, or more times as productive as the industry average. In fact, knowledge workers wanted to

---

[6] Speech delivered to a group of western managers and dignitaries. Quoted by Terry Hill in Manufacturing Strategy, 2nd ed. Irwin, p. 220, 1994.

be hired and paid depending on their talent, not the hours they would work on a given week.

It was as if manual workers had become a commodity, while talented knowledge workers marketed themselves as artists, usually "setting up shop" as freelancers!

The century-old carrot-and-stick motivational schemes started to tumble down with the arrival of these new kids, who wanted challenging problems to work at, unprecedented freedom to organize themselves, and a company they would be proud to work for. And doughnuts. In times of a strong job market, Lean experts even started to tell managers that they should treat their talented knowledge workers as volunteers if they wanted to retain them!

Taylor's Fateful Heritage: Dilbert, The Office, Office Space, and Other Cubicle Nightmares

Unfortunately, we still have lots of managers trained in the old-style hierarchical command-and-control stuff that are not suitable for the twenty-first-century challenges of managing such a workforce. Taylor's fateful heritage is still there, as old habits die hard, and many firms still treat these knowledge workers as commodities, try to standardize and control their work to the task level, and set individual bonuses based on spurious and arbitrary performance metrics.

There is a cultural clash out there. Managers trained on the Taylor-Ford methods use their power against people who are supposed to be creative problem solvers. Abuse of employees, harassment, arbitrary deadline setting, long hours, crunch time, public humiliation, lack of recognition, micromanagement, blaming, finger pointing, isolating, threatening, and other fear-based motivation-killing behaviors by managers are commonplace. We even had to create the verb "mobbing" to describe some of them.

In the software industry, where top-notch programmers can build magic and beat the industry average performance by orders of magnitude with unprecedented quality, we still see huge companies hiring programmers by the dozens, squeezing them until they drop dead, and then simply replacing them by fresh, new, undertrained recruits. Turnover rate is crazy, and projects are measured by how many hours we put on them, under the assumption that an hour in front of a keyboard is an hour of products produced. And if we put a million dollars worth of developers to produce some stupid thing nobody wants, that stupid thing nobody wants is supposed to be worth a million dollars.

This whole picture is what made the Dilbert comic strip one of the most successful in history. Featuring a corporate nightmare of incompetent bosses and hopeless, listless employees, Dilbert appears in 2,000 newspapers in 70 countries. It was the first syndicated comic strip to go online in 1995 and is the most widely read syndicated comic on the Internet.[7] From my perspective, Dilbert is a priceless repository of management anti-patterns for knowledge-based environments.

There are many other sources making fun of this crazy situation. For instance, the cult movie *Office Space* – tag lined "Work Sucks" – was a satire about the typical software company from the 1990s full of cubicles where talented employees spent days staring at their desks while evil managers abused and harassed them. In the movie, the only suitable solution to the decline of the company that managers can think of is downsizing – instead of solving the many flaws of the system, of course. Another well-known example of mockery of the typical end-of-the-twentieth-century workplace is the award-winning and many times replicated sitcom *The Office*. And there are plenty of other examples.

It is becoming clear for the knowledge-based society that this style of management is not bearable anymore, and we have to find a "new deal" between companies and talented workers in order to make the world a better place and build the next generation of great products and services.

That's what this book is about.

Summary

When the needs of the market grew beyond the capacity of what small guilds of craftsmen and artisans could produce, Taylor provided a good model to enable mass production of goods. In fact, Taylor's scientific management model is still a suitable way of managing production plants if you have an endless supply of cheap labor. That's why most emergent economies still rely on this model, with workers doing 14-h commutes 6 days a week.

---

[7] http://www.dilbert.com/about

Nevertheless, Japanese production methods based on high-value-adding workers have proven to be superior in terms of productivity, quality, innovation, and customer retention, so all sorts of first-world companies are striving to implement them as the only way to compete with emergent economies where labor is cheap and production costs are lower.

The rise of a knowledge-based economy introduced a new need to move from Taylor's command-and-control micromanagement model to collaboration-based comanagement where everyone's intelligence counts when it comes to improving the system. Workers not doing repetitive, algorithmic tasks but solving problems and being required to be creative and innovative in their solutions need a new space where they can develop their skills and talent to the most. Agile managers need to understand the particularity of such a workforce, how to motivate them and how to help them make the most out of themselves.

Things to Try

- Review the use of the term "leader" at your company: are you imposing leadership through a formal third-party appointment – for example, human resources hiring a "leader" for a team? Or is "leader" a title someone owns when he has shown the ability to lead others?

- Analyze the office politics of managers at your company. Does it seem like anyone is acting in his area's or department's best interest and against the general good of the company? If this is the case, you have a big chance of experiencing a feudal system, informal or not. Try to discuss this with the top management.

- Try to identify the parts of your business where people are really commodities, meaning that anyone will do and changing someone wouldn't make any kind of difference. Then think twice. If people in your company are not commodities, you have huge chance of improving if you implement a more Agile environment.

- Make a survey asking people you manage to rate the degree of Taylor versus Agile environment they are experiencing. You can use questions like "Are you allowed to make decisions regarding the way your work should be performed?" "Is your job perfectly defined?" "Do you feel like your opinion counts when it comes to decide how to manage work?" "Do you follow a constant, fixed process?" "Are you constantly supervised?"

or "Rate the degree of control you experience at work." Use the results to drive your Agile transformation process.

- Debate with your colleagues how productivity is measured in knowledge-based environments. For example, how do you compare the productivity of two software programmers? Lines of code? Hours? Features? How do you compare the productivity of two novelists? Is it all about the number of pages when it comes to market success? Research online about the topic. Try to question the way you are measuring productivity right now at your workplace and even if you should be making any productivity-oriented measurement.

- Think of the worst situations you've experienced at work (bad managers, chaotic projects, mergers, or acquisitions by arch rivals...). Try to describe what elements of fear and power abuse where present. Now think of the best work-related event you can remember – identify the motivational sources and any kind of fearless behavior involved.

- Ask your employees to choose their favorite Dilbert strip or maybe you can just find them hanging at their boards. Discuss with them how much your company behaves in a way similar to the one shown by the strip. If you find this useful, maybe you can arrange an afternoon show of *Office Space* with a debate afterward. Remember to bring lots of popcorn.

- Identify situations at your work environment where someone's criteria are imposed on others without participation or debate. Try to think on ways this could be performed in a more collaborative problem-solving way.

Recommended Readings

Drucker P (1996) Landmarks of tomorrow: a report on the new. Transaction Publishers, New Brunswick

Drucker P (2003) On the profession of management. Harvard Business Review Press, Boston

Drucker P (2008) The Essential Drucker: the best of sixty years of Peter Drucker's essential writings on management. HarperBusiness, New York

Ford H (2007) My life and work. Book Jungle

Jürgens U, Malsch T, Dohse K (2009) Breaking from Taylorism: changing forms of work in the automobile industry. Cambridge University Press, Cambridge

Ludwig AM (2002) King of the mountain: the nature of political leadership. The University Press of Kentucky, Lexington

Taylor FW (1997) The principles of scientific management. Dover Publications, Mineola

Van Vugt M, Ahuja A (2011) Naturally selected: the evolutionary science of leadership. HarperBusiness, New York

Lean and Agile in a Nutshell

2

Create Value, Eliminate Waste, and Adapt to Change

Agile and Lean

In Chap. 1, we started to develop the concept of "management" and "leadership" that you can read on the cover of this book. Now is the time to go into the "Agile" part of it.

In this (small) chapter, the basis of Agile and Lean will be reviewed to establish a common understanding and framework that allows further discussions. This book does not intend to be a comprehensive guide of what is Agile and Lean, nor a guide on how to implement Agile/Lean in your company, but I'll try to highlight the main implications of this concept for the organization and not only at the team level.

Again, this is not a book about Agile or Lean (oh my, I would need several books to explain those concepts deeply). But you can find some other excellent books on that topic out there. Some of the ones I recommend are those by Mary and Tom Poppendieck (Lean Software Development Series), Mike Cohn (specially the brilliant *Succeeding with Agile*), and Henrik Kniberg (*Scrum and XP from the Trenches*). And of course you can always engage in plenty of seminars and courses on the topic.

As many people (me included) consider that Agile is partly an evolution of Lean into the field of software/product development, I'll start with some background on Lean production.

Aichi Prefecture, Japan, 1946...

Á. Medinilla, *Agile Management*, DOI 10.1007/978-3-642-28909-5_2,
© Springer-Verlag Berlin Heidelberg 2012

The Japanese Revolution

In 1946, Toyota was a rather small car manufacturing plant in a country that had been devastated by World War II. The usual raw-material supply problems Japan had always experienced because of the fact of being an island in the middle of the Pacific Ocean were worsened by this situation, and the Americans transforming their mighty war production machinery into goods manufacturing plants were not helping, as they needed to sell those goods all around the world and were flooding markets with them (which explains the Marshall plan and other strategies for rebuilding Europe, but that is another story).

Furthermore, the country's morale was almost destroyed. After two atomic bombings, 3 million dead, 9 million homeless, the losing of the colonies, and the surrender of the nation by the Emperor, one would have expected the proud sons of the Samurai to commit collective ritual suicide or *Seppuku*.

But this is not what happened. Not at all. The Japanese reacted to this situation by bootstrapping the nation and devoting their millenary discipline to transform it as they had already done during the modernization in the Meiji period. This postwar rebirth of Japan was called the Showa era (1946–1989), and it has been repetitively referred to as "the Japanese miracle": building one of the most economically powerful countries of the world out of ashes and people's will. To address the magnitude of the change, realize that per capita income in Japan rose ten times between 1950 and 2008. And Toyota, for instance, became the world's biggest car manufacturer by 2007.

In fact, more than secret techniques, tools, or business plans, it was actually the collective effort and motivation of the workforce inspired by their leaders that made the whole transformation possible.

Management guru John Kotter dedicated several of his writings and studies to the figure of Konosuke Matsushita, and in his opinion, the start of the Japanese miracle can be traced back to the moment when, at the end of the war, he addressed his demoralized workforce and said, "I have been thinking about purpose." He then described a company that would force competitors to produce at the same outstanding levels of quality, innovation, and low prices that they will achieve, thus eliminating poverty in Japan and creating "a paradise on earth in the span of the next 250 years." It is been reported that several employees stood up in tears and said, "I think I could dedicate my life to this."

But let's go back to Toyota. By a similar process of continuous improvement and collective effort like the one going on in Matsushita, or even in the whole country, they designed a production system that was later studied by the Americans and baptized "Lean production." This system was based on a simple set of principles and rules that, when embraced by an engaged and empowered workforce, produced a plethora of tools, techniques, practices, artifacts, processes, roles, etc.

Unfortunately, for a long time, western companies tried to replicate those without really understanding the principles, which led to the rise of a set of approaches like Six Sigma, process reengineering, total quality, and other fads that tried to mimic the Japanese ways in a long-lasting, painful (and profitable) way of "Cargo Cult."

> "In the South Seas there is a cargo cult of people. During the war they saw airplanes land with lots of good materials, and they want the same thing to happen now. So they've arranged to imitate things like runways, to put fires along the sides of the runways, to make a wooden hut for a man to sit in, with two wooden pieces on his head like headphones and bars of bamboo sticking out like antennas – he's the controller – and they wait for the airplanes to land. They're doing everything right.
>
> The form is perfect. It looks exactly the way it looked before. But it doesn't work. No airplanes land. So I call these things cargo cult science, because they follow all the apparent precepts and forms of scientific investigation, but they're missing something essential, because the planes don't land."
>
> –Richard Feynman, *Cargo Cult Science*, 1974 Caltech commencement address

If you ever want to be successful on a Lean approach, please take your time to understand the basic rules and principles because those are the ones that you really have to plant on your soil: very probably, they will become some different kind of crop from the one the Japanese are harvesting, but it will be the one that suits your needs.

> "Copying practices without understanding the underlying principles has a long history of mediocre results. But when the underlying principles are understood, it is useful to copy practices that work for similar organizations and modify them to fit your environment."
>
> –Mary and Tom Poppendieck, *Lean Software Development*

The Five Principles of Lean

The whole Lean universe can be summarized in as few as five basic principles. Easy, right?

The first one is *understand and maximize value*. Very often, Lean is described as a way of "eliminating waste," but this is only a derivate of this principle. The hard part is trying to see your whole system as a way to produce value for your customer and truly understand how you provide that value.

Not everything your client pays for is value, and on many occasions, companies are dead wrong about how their client sees the value of the product.

For example, at a meeting on a very well-known drill-machines manufacturer, the CEO asked the management board "Gentlemen, what it is that we sell to our clients here?" Everyone, as expected, replied, "The best possible, most powerful, cheapest, highest quality drill machines in the world." But the CEO replied, "nonsense! You don't understand this company! Holes! Holes in a wall is what we sell!"

The CEO understood a deep truth about what their client valued. If there was a better way of making holes in a wall than using a drill machine, the company was wasting its efforts on building better drill machines. Because this is not what their clients truly valued.

Once you understand value, you can start looking at the whole company and asking yourself "how is this activity adding value to our client?" It is a dangerous question to make to yourself because you will realize that many of the things lying around your plant are not directly contributing to your client's experience. And then, on a Lean environment, they have to be labeled as "waste" and you have to strive to reduce them to the minimum or even eliminate them.

For me, the magical question you have to make to identify waste is, "are we willing to do more of this? Like, for example, double it?" With this question, you'll rapidly realize that meetings, managers, reports, inventories, transportations, rework, handoffs, overproduction, delays, and many other kinds of "wastes" are things that you have to eliminate or reduce to the minimum – but not less than the minimum, of course.

> "Make things as simple as possible, but not simpler."
>
> –Albert Einstein

Many times managers feel discomfort when I label management as "waste," but be honest to yourself: if management is true "value" for your client, are you willing to double the number of managers on your company? Maybe triple it?

Do you prefer to fly with one company or another depending on which one has the most managers?

No, you want to have the minimum viable number of managers that works for your company. And then find the way to work with even less managers.

The second principle of Lean is *optimize the value stream.* That means understanding how the different activities of your company contribute to producing value and then finding the way to place them on a sequence that shortens the production cycle, hence reducing both cycle time (time to produce a feature from work start to end) and the lead time (elapsed time since the feature was actually asked for by the client).

A very popular tool to implement this second principle is value stream mapping. To implement a value stream map for your company, just take a pencil and some paper (experts stress the importance of not using software and doing this by hand) and start from the end, that is, the value delivery to your customer. Then start tracing back where this value came from, how much did it take, what effort was put into it, how much of this effort was actually waste, and how much was value-adding activities. Then repeat and continue until you arrive at the place where your client order was received. If you divide the value-adding time by the total time – including queues, delays, waiting periods, and non-value-adding activities – you'll have a performance ratio indicator of your process. For companies that haven't been through a Lean initiative, performance ratios of 9–20% are not unusual. If you do your first Value Stream Map and you obtain something above 50%, don't congratulate yourself too much – you have to look twice, possibly with the help of an expert.

Optimizing the value stream is not only a matter of mapping, measuring, and reducing: it is a crucial exercise to understand and see your company as a whole, not as independent black boxes each of them trying to do the best for themselves. As systems engineering teaches us, any attempt to optimize one part of the system will very probably suboptimize the whole.

"The obligation of any component is to contribute its best to the system, not to maximize its own production, profit, or sales nor any other competitive measure. Some components may operate at a loss to themselves in order to optimize the whole system, including the components that take a loss."

–Edward Deming, *The New Economics*

The third Lean principle is *pull production*. This means that new products are only manufactured when the client needs them, reducing the need of stocks, inventories, or in-excess production. Small stocks are maintained, and when one piece is consumed, another one is immediately produced to replace it. For this to work, the system must be able to change their production and deliver very fast to react to the needs of their clients, thus embracing change and uncertainty. Any attempt at "Manufacturing Resource Planning" or "yearly forecasts" is an anathema for a Lean industry.

Lean skeptics will argue that some kind of planning is needed, and that is absolutely true. But in a world where something like Facebook appears and makes 50 million clients in less than 2 years, there is a need to react faster than a year's time. Planning and executing cycles must be reduced to the minimum possible, and that is why most software industries in the Agile or Lean startup frameworks are moving to 2-week production cycles of plan, execute, release, and collect feedback.

For instance, the whole design and production of the Toyota Prius, a new concept hybrid engine car, took Toyota roughly a year, when the industry average for a new regular model of car was 4–5 years. And we are talking of 1997 here. Nowadays, the Spanish company Inditex is able to deliver clothes to any store worldwide in 72 hours, thus reducing the need of huge stocks at the stores and being able to react when some particular model is selling well by increasing the production of that particular model. The contrary is also true: if some model is not selling, the most you are losing is 3 days of production of that model, as there is no need to produce millions in advance without actually knowing if someone will even look at it.

For the third principle to work, the fourth principle is needed: *single-piece flow*, defined as the ability of a single order or piece of work to flow smoothly across the whole system without interruptions and at the maximum possible speed. This usually implies reducing the amount of things going on at a particular moment, as Little's law establishes that cycle time increases with the amount of pieces on the system. In other words, the more things you think you are doing at the same time, the less productive you become.

This means that multitasking is a myth, as is the "total productivity." In his book *Quality Software Management: Systems Thinking*, Gerald Weinberg measured the performance of an individual working on several projects: compared to working with a single project, the loss of productivity because of context switching was as much as 40% for someone working simultaneously in three projects and 75% for someone at five projects! This is the reason why Kanban systems' main rule is to limit the work in progress (WIP), with an ideal goal of WIP limit "one," meaning that you don't start another task until this one is finished, even if it gets blocked. This idea of "focusing on the next actionable item" and not starting anything else until this one is finished is also one of the bases of the very popular "Getting Things Done" or GTD personal productivity and time management system by David Allen.

Finally, the fifth and my personal favorite Lean principle is *continuous improvement*, or in Japanese *"Kaizen."* – a hopeless but joyful strive for perfection that makes us better every day. Today, better than yesterday. Tomorrow, better than today. A martial state of mind that makes us train constantly and never be satisfied with our current skill, no matter how high it is.

> "This old man must still train and train"
>
> –O Sensei Morihei Ueshiba, Aikido founder, declared "Sacred National Treasure" of Japan, one of the greatest martial artists of its time, at the age of 86, shortly before he passed away.[1]

Again, Lean skeptics will try to argue that "perfection is impossible" or even say "why do we want to be better? We are just fine now. ..." But on a Lean environment, there is a perpetual state of discomfort with the current state. Lean leaders will constantly push the organization out of its zone of comfort in search of a new, higher level of quality, performance, and, overall, client satisfaction.

---

[1] Ueshiba M, Ueshiba K (1996) Budo: teachings of the Founder of Aikido Ueshiba. Kodansha International, p 21.

"What's perfection good for if we will never reach it? It gives us a true
north so we keep walking on its direction"

–Anonymous banner at the 15-M revolts in Madrid, 2011[2]

The 14 Principles of the Toyota Production System

Dr. Jeffrey Liker presented a deeper insight on Lean production systems in
his 2004 book *The Toyota Way*. He summarized 14 principles and behaviors
that described Toyota's managerial approach to Lean production:

1. *Base your management decisions on a long-term philosophy, even at the
   expense of short-term financial goals.* There is always an urge somewhere, a fire elsewhere, and something critical to be done anywhere else,
   but you have to understand that there will always be. So if you start
   dropping trainings, holidays, market events, innovation workshops, or
   improvement programs because of delivery dates, you are investing in
   short-term goals and creating an ever-growing learning debt. In a Lean
   environment, provided we have enough resources to invest and provided
   this investment will not ruin the company in the short term, we will
   always try to invest in long-term improvement, learning, and growing,
   even at the price of short-term losses.

2. *Create a continuous process flow to bring problems to the surface.*
   Searching for new forms of waste and ways to reducing it shall not be
   limited to a certain number of "Kaizen events." A regular process must be
   put in place instead, and management must make sure that all problems
   detected by the workforce and tagged as "waste" or "impediments" are
   urgently addressed as national emergencies, even if it means delaying
   short-term projects (first principle).

3. *Use "pull" systems to avoid overproduction.* This was one of the five
   original lean principles and was so reflected by Liker in "The Toyota
   Way." The pull and flow principles led to the revolutionary "just-in-time
   production" concept, meaning that pieces and products were only delivered exactly when needed, thus reducing the need of inventories, warehouse space, and other forms of waste.

---

[2] As seen by myself.

4. *Level out the workload (heijunka)*. Instead of bursts of work followed by periods of lower activity, try to achieve a sustainable pace and a constant production rate. Variability of demand can be absorbed by small production buffers (sometimes called heijunka boxes), producing in small batches (hence being able to adapt better to a changing demand) and achieving low die change times (being able to change between the production of two different pieces very quickly and at a low cost).

5. *Build a culture of "stop the line*," which means that when a problem is detected, it is more important to stop production and fix the problem, making sure that we will never make the same mistake again, than continuing the production and making a mental note of "we should be fixing this later on." Stopping the production line has a short-term cost, but the implication in the long term is huge. Maintaining a pile of defects, problems, impediments, and inefficiencies creates a "compound interest" effect on quality, thus creating a "technical debt." Some examples of "stop the line" culture are *Andon* devices, a red-light signal that tells management that a problem has been detected and the line needs to be stopped, and *Jidoka* or "autonomation," automation with a human touch, which means that the whole product line can be stopped automatically when a machine automatically stops and a human supervisor decides that the problem must be addressed. In software companies, these principles have been implemented in the form of automatic test, build, and deploy systems that tell the programmers when something went wrong during the automated process.

6. *Standardize work*, but not in the way western companies understood it during the 1980s and the 1990s. Toyota understood standardized work as a tool to make sure that everyone was doing things the same way, so when they changed something, they could measure the effects of that change and evaluate if it was a good idea or not. It was also a way for every worker to know what he was expected to do. But workers were responsible for constantly reviewing the standard in search of better ways to perform, and managers were accountable for it. It is said that Taiichi Ohno, considered one of the fathers of the Toyota Production System, fired a manager because the standard that his team was following had not been changed in more than a year. Please make sure you understand this: standards must change constantly. Otherwise we are considering that we have found the perfect way of working, which is by definition not possible, or we consider that this way is good enough for us, which is against the principle of continuous improvement.

7. *Use visual control so no problems are hidden.* Again, western companies will always come up with software tools, written reports, or electronic dashboards to try to know what is happening, but according to the general experience of Lean and Agile *Senseis*, nothing beats the simplicity of visual controls. Kanban cards, team boards, signs, banners, *Andon* devices, A3 handwritten reports, floor layout lines, or silhouetted tool boxes where you can easily know where to place everything are typical examples of visual management in a Lean manufacturing plant. Visual control devices also foster team collaboration, employee empowerment, and a sense of ownership that no electronic tool has been able to reproduce.

8. *Use only reliable, thoroughly tested technology that serves your people and processes.* Align technology with your process and not the other way round. Technology must help your people do things easier, faster, and in a more efficient way. If the technology you are using is making people hate it, you are probably serving some needs other than the one of your people and your process. Or your process is darn wrong!

9. *Grow leaders who thoroughly understand the work, live the philosophy, and teach it to others.* There is no better way to teach people than personal example. Lean leaders are a living incarnation of the Lean principles and values, who feel that their main responsibility is to make everyone understand the company's culture. Japanese Lean Senseis often say that the main problem with western managers is that they want to rule and command, not to teach.

> "We must become the change we want to see in the world."
>
> –Mahatma Gandhi

10. *Develop exceptional people and teams who follow your company's philosophy.* Again, the Lean concept around people is to make them responsible for the process. Empowerment and ownership are frequent terms when describing people's behavior in a Lean environment. As stated in the previous principle, Lean leaders are devoted not to command and control their people but to inspire the purpose, principles, and values that lead to the desired results.

"If you want to build a ship, don't drum up the men to gather wood, divide the work and give orders. Instead, teach them to yearn for the vast and endless sea."

—Antoine de Saint-Exupery

11. *Respect your extended network of partners and suppliers by challenging them and helping them improve.* The supply chain is not to be considered a zero-sum game where everything that your supplier is earning is something that you are losing. By developing a trust relationship with your partners and helping them improve, you are improving your own process, and joint ventures between suppliers and clients based on this kind of trust have proved to systematically produce amazing results and long-term win-win situations.

12. *Go and see for yourself to thoroughly understand the situation.* Often translated as "management by wandering," *Genchi Genbutsu* is an important practice for the Lean leader: don't rely only on reports, metrics, scorecards, and meetings. Go where the action is. Live with your team, sit with them, and experiment by yourself what is happening at the *Gemba*, the place where work is being performed. Help your team perform better and instruct them at the workplace. By the way, if you are not able to personally train your people, you are probably not qualified to be a true Lean leader and are working under the old Taylor paradigms of thinking managers versus working labor instead.

13. *Make decisions slowly by consensus, thoroughly considering all options,* and then implement decisions rapidly (*Nemawashi*). Incorporating everyone's opinion in the decision-making process can be hard, but once again this short-term investment produces great long-term results: a more committed workforce, better decisions based on a more complete view of the system, enhanced collaboration, and less conflicts.

14. *Become a learning organization through relentless reflection (Hansei) and continuous improvement (Kaizen).* The master principle of Lean: never be satisfied with your current state, strive for perfection. Every mistake is seen as an opportunity to improve as long as people are empowered to take risks, make mistakes, and learn from them. Blame-avoiding games will never make the company better, they will only keep you safe, and trying to ignore mistakes is another form of blame avoiding. In a Hansei-Kaizen culture, everyone feels responsible and accountable for their decisions, and when a mistake has been made, it is

more important to fix it and make sure that no one else will make the same mistake again than trying to hide the broken glass under the carpet.

Over these 14 principles, constant improvement and respect for people remained as the foundations to correctly implement them, and this remains the base of Toyota's competitive advantage.

Kanban Systems

The five master principles (Value, Value Stream, Pull, Flow, Kaizen) and the "Toyota Way" 14 principles gave birth to a plethora of practices and tools that have been deeply covered by the Lean literature. We've already mentioned Jidoka, Andon, Heijunka, Value Stream Mapping, Genchi Genbutsu, Just-in-Time, Gemba Kaizen, A3 reports... And there is more: You can read about *Poka-Yoke* or foolproof design (e.g., the USB connector that can only be plugged one way); *5S plant maintenance systems* (Sort-Set in order-Shine-Standardize-Sustain); *Single-Minute Exchange of Die*, or the ability to change from one product manufacturing to another very fast; *or root cause analysis* as a way to look at problems, often combined with *Ishikawa fishbone diagrams.*

As you see, we would need a whole dictionary to describe all the tools and practices that the Lean enterprises have produced in the last decades as forms to implement the 5 root principles and the 14 Toyota Way principles. But one of them is especially important because of its relevance that has been recognized recently in the IT industry: *Kanban systems.*

> "The two pillars of the Toyota production system are just-in-time production and automation with a human touch, or autonomation. The tool used to operate the system is kanban."
>
> –Taiichi Ohno, *The Toyota Production System*

Modern Kanban authors like David J. Anderson make a difference between "kanban," a tool to manage demand, and "Kanban," with a capital "K," a framework to look at production systems, spot bottlenecks, and trigger employee empowerment and continuous improvement.

The original idea behind Kanban systems is to attach a physical card – or kanban – to any piece of work being done at the factory and then limit the amount of available kanbans to match the production capacity. Thus, any order coming when no kanbans are available has to wait on a buffer until some resources are released. If demand is higher than capacity, the buffers will start to grow, and this will be understood as a need to rearrange the system so it is able to cope with the growing demand.

This can be achieved by adding more resources, of course, but it is usually possible to raise the capacity also by improving the production process, eliminating waste, removing impediments, training people, improving quality... Companies that directly add more resources whenever they have a peak of demand have ever-growing costs, and their quality remains the same or worse, while companies that strive to improve their system reduce their costs, raising their production capacity and their product quality.

Kanban systems also provide a simple way to "see the whole" by gathering all the kanban cards at a given moment and putting them on a board that represents the production process. Measuring the time a kanban takes to move from one production step to another, we can obtain valuable information on cycle time (the time a single unit takes to be produced since we start working on it) or lead time (same, but counting from the time the order entered the system). We can also see where the kanbans are stopping and growing queues, or even where a production cell is running out of work.

For example, look at this simple kanban board for a software development team of four people. Every kanban represents a piece of work that has to be designed, coded, and tested, so the flow of work is represented from left to right. Small comic-like avatars are also used to represent the people working at them:

It is easy to see that the poor guy on the test column has a lot of "code ready" kanbans to work on. Of course we could add more testers. But maybe the problem is that the "code ready" code is not as ready as the coders think, so maybe we should invest our resources better by training the coders and asking them to spend more time on their work until the quality of the code is enough for a smooth testing. This would have both the effects of reducing the throughput of the coders and making the tester work faster, as he would have better quality materials to work at. So we would have equalized the system without introducing new costs in the form of more – demoralized – testers. As you can see, the visualization of the value stream and the work in progress help us understand the whole and improve the system.

A true Kanban system works with a simple set of rules:

1. Start by doing exactly what you are doing right now.
2. Map the value stream.
3. Visualize all work on the value stream by adding kanban cards.
4. Introduce work-in-progress (WIP) limits.
5. Help the system flow and improve everything.

The WIP limits are usually one of the most difficult steps when implementing a Kanban system. We have been trained on the myth of "multitasking": doing several things at the same time as a way of being more efficient. But, in fact, reality works the other way round: the less things you are doing in parallel, the more efficiently you will perform them. When you switch between two or more tasks, there is an inherent loss of capacity due to context switching, and the more things you are switching between, the longer it takes to finish every single one of them.

This has been proven by examples, mathematics, simulations, real cases, and many other ways, but still we tend to bite more than we can chew and open as many tasks as possible, as if it was making us more productive. Kanban systems provide a tool to control this trend and, thus, improve both capacity and lead time. For Kanban and WIP limits to work, a small batch size is needed. Small batches are, hence, one of the paradigms of the Lean production systems, allowing fast exchange of product lines, low WIP limits, lower lead times, etc.

When you look at true Kanban systems, you realize that they address the need to understand value, see the whole value stream, help the system flow, work under pull events, and improve the whole. So Kanban is possibly the simplest way to implement the five root principles of Lean with a single tool!

Again, this is not a book on Agile or Lean tools, but you will find very valuable resources on Kanban and other Lean tools at the end of this chapter.

The NUMMI Experiment: Lean Everywhere

At the beginning of the studies on the Japanese production methods, some Lean skeptics argued that this kind of productivity was only possible in Japanese environments, where the workforce was so alienated and submissive that they will work themselves to death. Well, in fact, there is a Japanese word for that: *karoshi...*

Some other skeptics claimed that the Japanese competitive advantage was due to a devaluated yen, while others pointed at superior automation. But all these arguments were silenced after the NUMMI experiment.

At the beginning of the 1980s, General Motors was having big trouble with the NUMMI manufacturing plant in Fremont, California. It was described by company officials as "one of the worst in the industry": the absenteeism was so high that sometimes the whole plant shut down because there were not enough people to operate it, and frequently workers came drunk to work and sabotaged the cars they were making with small pranks, like placing beer cans inside the frame so they would rattle while driving. Quality was awful, costs were outrageous, and capacity was embarrassingly low.

General Motors ended up closing the plant in 1982. But in those times, Toyota was looking for a way to better introduce their products in the United States, and General Motors was also eager to know more about the Toyota Production System. So the two companies reopened the plant in 1984 as a joint venture – with 85% of the original workforce.

You can imagine the faces of the General Motors managers when, few years later, Fremont's NUMMI plant started assembling cars in 19 h (instead of GM's average of 31), with 45 defects per 100 cars (instead of GM's average 130), operating with 2 h of inventory (instead of GM's average of 2 weeks), no space for rework (instead of GM's average of 15%), and with no absenteeism at all (instead of GM's average of 15%).

GM was shocked. And the most shocking fact was that the whole workforce was hired from the former NUMMI workers, but *virtually no former top manager was rehired*. That means that management was Japanese and workforce was American.

When Toyota Lean Senseis were asked about this fact, they simply replied "the problem with your managers is that they want to rule, command and control, not to teach." Furthermore, observers described the way Japanese managers collaborated with American workers as "comanagement."

So yes, Lean can be implemented everywhere, and yes, management can be the big difference – or the big impediment – when trying to implement and improve a Lean system. If you tend to look around and say to yourself "oh, that would never work here," try to imagine a drunken American car worker placing beer cans inside the product, and try to explain how worse is your situation right now.

Lean in a Nutshell

Summarizing Lean in a couple of pages is a lost-in-advance battle, but I'll try to give some ideas on how a Lean system feels like. . ..

A Lean system is devoted to understand how we produce value from a customer perspective and then arrange all our processes and activities in a way that creates the most value and minimizes waste. Products are developed just in time with the minimum possible amount of time, space, and costs. There is a constant effort in lowering production time as a way to increase productivity and suit best the needs of the customer.

Work flows in small batches from the beginning of the production line without stop, and bottlenecks are rapidly addressed to maintain the line flow. The work in progress is limited to a certain amount, with "single-piece flow" (meaning that you only work on one thing at a time) being the ideal state.

Work is standardized not as a way to increase bureaucracy but as a common arrangement of how things should be done. When a problem or impediment is detected, everyone in the plant is empowered to take risks, stop the line, and swarm around the problem to not only solve it now, but also make sure that this problem will never rise again. Standards of work are updated constantly to include the solutions to the detected problems, and the whole system is constantly improved.

There are neither individual competitions nor blame-avoiding games, as everyone is aligned in the aim of improving the whole. Errors are tolerated and seen as an opportunity to improve, so there is no fear to take risks or point out mistakes. Work groups self-organize to find the best way to optimize the system by experimenting and innovating in inspect-and-adapt cycles.

Visual boards are available everywhere so the state of work and any possible issues are detected as fast as possible and seen by everyone in the plant. Managers are available for work groups, and they will help them understand the job to be done and remove any impediments for them. They will also help them raise any issue to the company level and reach their full potential.

> "The fundamental principle of successful management is to allow subordinates to make full use of their ability"
>
> –Kaoru Ishikawa's *What is Totally Quality Control? The Japanese Way*

Quality is seen not only as conformance to requirements that has to be tested at the end of the line. A holistic approach to quality is embraced, and everyone is responsible for building quality into the whole process.

Kaizen events are frequent, and everyone in the company is required to contribute to the innovation and continuous improvement of both the product and the system. Company strategy in the long term is honored on daily short-term decisions, even at the expense of short-term losses, and this long-term thinking is also applied to company development, training, improvement, and constant reflection (Hansei).

The Pre-Manifesto Years: Agile Genealogy

Unfortunately, while the car industry was changing the world of manufacturing into Lean production, the information technology or IT industry was not catching up.

For decades, the paradigm of "software engineering" rested on the foundation of perfectly defining what was to be built and then starting to build it, which seems logical on a first thought. Hence, a huge number of methods and disciplines were designed to define, estimate, and plan software development before a single line of code was written. The worse the results, the more the software industry tried to introduce even more documents, specifications, timetables, schedules, processes, milestones, etc.

And the results were bad. Standish Group, a Boston-based project management and consulting firm, started to periodically release the "Chaos Report" about the state of project management in the IT industry. The report is based on hundreds of cases, and the underlying premise is, paraphrasing 1986's president of Transarc Corporation Alfred Spector, that bridges are normally built on time, on budget, and do not fall down, but, on the other hand, software never comes in on time or on budget and, in addition, it always breaks down.[3]

In fact, the numbers repetitively shown by Chaos Reports are scary: according to the participants, in 2009, only 32% of all projects succeeded (were delivered on time, on budget, with required features and functions), while 44% were challenged (late, over budget, and/or with less than the required features and functions) and 24% failed (canceled or delivered and never used).[4] Furthermore, the Standish reports consistently show as low as 50 or 60 cents of value delivered for every dollar spent on software, meaning that half the cost of building software is what Lean Senseis call "waste."

Still, the software industry's standard response for three decades has been "we have to estimate better – if we make perfect estimations, then our projects will always be on time, on budget and will have all the required functionality; if bridge builders can estimate, why can't we?"

At the same time, a few IT projects were beating the industry's average performance by several orders of magnitude. Small teams of no more than eight people were capable of delivering thousands of lines of working software – every week! Experts started to trace and study those projects, and what they found there was against all the established lore in IT project management. These teams were self-organizing to produce working software on short iterations, obtaining frequent feedback from the client and then rapidly adapting and extending the working software to the new requirements. Quality was outstanding, and several strategies were used to automate as many parts of the process as possible, including testing, building, and deployment. A new set of practices and tools started to emerge from those teams, including pair programming, short releases, automated building and testing, test-driven development, etc.

---

[3] Sachs I (2011) CHAOS report. In: Performance-driven IT management: five practical steps to business success. Government Institutes.

[4] Standish Group Press release, http://www.standishgroup.com/newsroom/chaos_2009.php

So we had some people empirically experimenting the first principles and practices of Agile Software Development. But it was not the only path that guided some brilliant pioneers to the concept. Some of them started by analyzing the Lean body of knowledge and bumped into a seminal paper by Ikujiro Nonaka and Hirotaka Takeuchi: *The New New Product Development Game*.[5] In this 1986 paper, Nonaka and Takeuchi proposed that it wasn't enough anymore to have a good product at a good price to survive – it was also necessary to adapt to an ever-changing demand from customers who now required companies to evolve their products constantly, and it was also necessary to be able do it fast! Nonaka and Takeuchi found that companies following a "waterfall" methodology of development – meaning that requirements, design, building, testing, and delivery were sequential phases usually performed by different groups of people – were not achieving the best results.

Instead, cross-functional teams of people with different skill sets that were iterating and adapting requirements, design, building, and deployment at the same time were achieving the best results in terms of creativity, innovation, productivity, quality, and time to market. Nonaka and Takeuchi compared the two approaches to a relay race, where the project was the baton and was handed from one group to another at the end of each phase, and a rugby scrum, where the project was the rugby ball and the whole team pushed it further.

In the 1990s, other experts started to apply Queue Theory and Theory of Constraints to software development, dividing the project in small batches and trying to move them through the development process as fast as they could removing bottlenecks. This was of course inspired by the Lean practices of flow and pull.

Simultaneously, some scientists studying complexity science theorized that software development is a complex field, meaning that requirements are not stable: they change when the client starts to use the product and finds new needs or discards functionality that he originally thought he needed, or even change because the environment and the problem constantly change while the software is being developed, and thus, a predictive method of requirements gathering and full solution design is not adequate: an inspect-and-adapt or empirical method should be used to approach software

---

[5] Nonaka I, Takeuchi H (1986) The new product development game. Harvard Business Review 65(1):137–144.

development as a complex problem, and products should be built iteratively and incrementally.

A whole new set of methodologies and frameworks started to emerge. Some of the most important were eXtreme Programming (XP), Scrum, Feature-Driven Development (FDD), Crystal Methodologies, or Dynamic Systems Development Method (DSDM).

The Agile Manifesto

In February of 2001, after more than two decades of research and practice, 17 of these experts gathered together in Utah and wrote the Agile Software Development Manifesto.[6] First seen as a countermovement against documentation-driven, heavyweight software development processes, the Manifesto was the foundation for a huge movement that, today, is widely considered the better way to develop software. Even today, a decade later, the Manifesto is still considered by many as the ultimate guide and assessment to see how Agile your software development process is.

The Manifesto reads:

> "We are uncovering better ways of developing
> software by doing it and helping others do it.
> Through this work we have come to value:
>
> –Individuals and interactions over processes and tools
> –Working software over comprehensive documentation
> –Customer collaboration over contract negotiation
> –Responding to change over following a plan
>
> That is, while there is value in the items on
> the right, we value the items on the left more."
>
> –Manifesto for Agile Software Development (17 signatories)

Let me give you my own view of the Manifesto.

As you see, the Manifesto starts by acknowledging the existence of many ways of doing things, but, in the opinion of the Agilists, Agile is a better

---

[6] http://www.agilemanifesto.org

way. That means you can still build a great product even if you don't use Agile. For me, this first part of the Manifesto is what I like to call "the great promise of Agile," which is that no matter how bad things go, the worst thing that can happen if you go Agile is to end up having the same results you had in the beginning.

The Manifesto goes on stating that we are uncovering these better ways by doing it, meaning this is not just an academic exercise, we've been doing this stuff and eating our own dog food and helping others do it, which means that this is not something that only works for us; you can do it too!

Then, the Manifesto enumerates the four foundational values of Agile development, but please keep in mind the last phrase: we value the items on the right! Agile is not a chaotic commune of software hippies demanding to ban documents, processes, contracts, tools, and plans. In fact, too many people have seen the Agile movement as a war between good developers and bad managers, and that is absolutely not the case. You only have to read the principles to find the need of software developers and business people to collaborate daily on the project.

The four values start with "individuals and interactions over processes and tools." As said, this is not a call to ban processes and tools: software development is a knowledge-sharing game, and the best way of managing knowledge is through personal interactions. Processes and tools must be designed keeping this fact in mind and they should foster communication, interaction . . .and face-to-face communication. If they keep people out of this kind of interactions, asking to fill timesheets, knowledge-based wikis, and a whole bunch of procedural forms instead, then they should be redesigned.

The second value is "working software over comprehensive documenta-tion." Project documentation, from an Agile-Lean perspective, is waste. More project documentation does not give more functionality or value to the customer, so we should try to have as few documentation as possible – but not less! Spending the first few months of a project writing documents is not the best way of providing value to our customer, when we could be designing prototypes, proof of concepts, or technical spikes instead and evolving them into the full product in short client-driven iterations.

The third value is "customer collaboration over contract negotiation." Of course, contracts are important. But even when you are protected by a contract, if your client finds new needs and you don't put them into the product because your contract does not require you to do so, you are not providing the most possible value to your client. If both parts accept that project will change and they are fine with that, a better way of collaborating and building products will be reached.

This acceptance of change is also present in the fourth value: responding to change over following a plan. Planning is important but only as far as you understand that the plan will be outdated immediately, and you have to constantly adapt to a changing environment. This is a basic principle of the universe that you have to admit to be a successful manager: you can adapt your project to reality – trying to adapt reality to your project will not work.

> "In preparing for battle I have always found that plans are useless, but planning is indispensable."
>
> –Dwight David Eisenhower, American 34th President (1953–1961)

Principles of Agile Development

The Agile Manifesto also lists 12 principles for Agile Software Development, but going in depth into each of them is out of the scope of this book. Instead, I'll give you the 10-min abstract I used to show on my seminars after six hours of Agile principles dissection.

Try to imagine traditional software development like this:

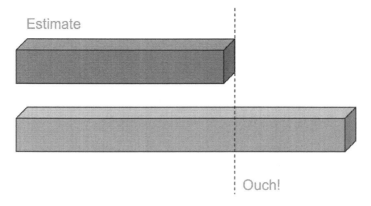

As you can see, you do some initial planning, come up with some crazy estimates, draw an aggressive deadline, and start coding like there is no tomorrow. Some weeks before the deadline timid voices start to question it, and pessimistic reports arrive asking for more time because of unexpected events, faulty materials, wrong requirements... Oh, yes, and the client is making changes. Too many changes. So you move the deadline and prepare yourself to receive hell from both client and boss. There is nothing else to do, except urging everyone to do long hours – it is crunch time, and now you are on a death-march project!

This lowers morale and has a bad effect on product quality, which also contributes to new delays, and so not only your project is doomed: your next project will suffer from the constant interruptions, support tickets, and trouble reports that this project will cause in the future.

Now try to imagine a different reality:

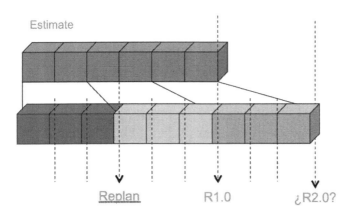

This time you started with the same estimate you had in the other case, but now you focused on delivering the 33% of most important features (the first ones) as soon as possible. So maybe on month 3, you had a first prototype consisting of the three most important groups of features, or "epics." You realize then that they were supposed to have ended by month 2, so you clearly detect that estimates were very optimistic and it is time to replan.

What shall we do? Well, now that we are releasing working features regularly, there are more options. For instance, we could release "something" on the deadline (release 1.0) and then release the full product later (release 2.0).

But if we are delivering the most important features first, then the last features consist of the "nice to have" or "could-wish" part of the product. Maybe the cost of extending the project 3 months past the original deadline is not worth the business value we will get from these features.

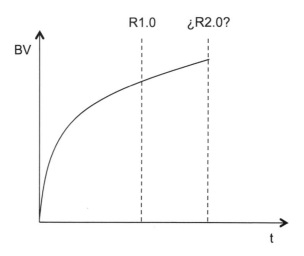

This is a decision to be made by business people. In the worst case, releasing a product with only 66% of the most important features will not be acceptable to the client, but then, we would be in the first case again! So, as promised by the Manifesto, the worst thing that can happen is to finish up exactly as you were before implementing Agile. But, on the way, Agile has given you a new series of options you did not have before – like start using the 66% of the most important features before the final release.

Also, having a working product as soon as possible helps the client see what he actually needs, thus having better information than when you ask him to write on a document what he will need in the future. This has the effect of reducing risks and uncertainty, usually reducing the project time and improving the quality of the product and the satisfaction of our client.

The principles of the Manifesto describe this kind of development, where the main metric of progress is not the time elapsed, percentage of the Gantt chart done, or number of working hours put into the project, but working software delivered. Working software is the primary measure of progress, and the features we deliver are prioritized in order to satisfy our customer needs, so the most important features are delivered first. These deliveries to the customer are done on short time scales, from a couple of weeks to a couple of months, and the delivered product should be as close to production state as possible. Every delivery creates an opportunity for our client to test the software, change the requirements, and replan the whole project, something we welcome as a way to provide competitive advantage to him.

The Agile principles establish that this kind of process must be performed by a motivated, self-organizing team of developers that is collaborating daily with business people, works at a sustainable pace, actively seeks face-to-face communication, strives for technical excellence, and frequently reflects on how to improve, simplify, maximize value, and reduce waste.

Easy, right?

Again: From Values and Principles to Practices and Tools

As we saw when studying Lean, just trying to copy the practices and tools will not take the company to a Lean state. The same happens with Agile: just trying to put some post-it notes around and conduct daily meetings will not make you Agile. Only the constant effort to embrace the values and the principles will. If you guide your company through the values and the principles in the Manifesto, it does not matter if you are doing Scrum, XP, Kanban, Lean Software Development, or the last fancy flavor of Agile. That is why, lately, many Agilists are urging companies to stop *doing* Agile and *be* Agile instead.

Anyway, the implementation of the Agile values and principles, as well as the previous work done by the Agile pioneers, has produced a well-documented set of best practices that very possibly will help you understand and embrace Agile. Some of them are described below, but, again, let me stress that even if you start performing all of them, that will not necessarily make you Agile.

From my own perspective, Agile companies must understand values and principles first and then try to find the set of processes, roles, practices, artifacts, and tools that help them live by those values and principles *and not the other way round*. There are outstanding Agile software tools out there that will help you manage your projects, collaborate with other developers, automate your testing, building, and deployment, or even measure the quality of your code. Be sure none of them will *make you Agile*. Here is some advice: If you can spend some resources on the Agile adoption process, be sure to spend it on people and not on software.

Some Agile Practices and Tools

Please be sure to read the previous section before going on. Twice. Now, you are encouraged to use as many of these practices as possible, as they have proven to be very useful and rewarding, not only to help Agile adoption but to improve team collaboration and overall performance in all kinds of projects:

- *Cross-functional teams*: Instead of setting up a team of analysts, a team of developers, and a team of testers, try to make a team of 5–9 people that includes analysts, coders, and testers. Then ask them to collaborate and produce working software together every couple of weeks, which will probably force the analysts to do some testing or the testers to do some coding. Be sure to measure and rank the team as a whole depending on the main measure of progress: working software delivered! This will introduce some problems with hyper-specialists or people whose skills are seldom used and may not have enough work to do in a team of 5–9: we will deal with this in the chapter about Agile structures.

- *Iterative and incremental development*: Instead of building block A, and then block B, and then block C, only to find out that nothing really works until block Z is in place, try to deliver a small working version of the system as soon as possible. Try to live by the philosophy of "Release early, release often and listen to your customers" proposed by Eric S. Raymond in his essay "The Cathedral and the Bazaar".[7] Several approaches have been proposed for this, including Alistair Cockburn's walking skeleton or the Minimum Marketable Feature Set/Minimum Viable Product concept.

- *Daily meetings*: Meetings are often seen as a terrible waste of time. The solution is not to have fewer meetings (well, maybe just a few less) but to be more efficient in their moderation and facilitation. On the other hand, in groups of people often called "teams," it is not rare to find individuals who don't know what their colleagues are doing in any given moment and think that they only have to worry about their personal bit of stuff. A daily five to ten minutes face-to-face meeting where every team member reports his activities, progress, and impediments is a great way of both updating the information about the project, better knowing our

---

[7] Raymond ES (1999) The cathedral and the bazaar: musings on Linux and open source by an accidental revolutionary. O'Reilly Media.

colleagues, sharing knowledge, showing some interest, fostering collaboration, and growing better teams.

- *Feature-Driven Development*: If we have to deliver working software every 2 weeks or so, a high stress has to be put on developing working features as a whole, instead of spending some months designing the architecture, then another few months developing the core, then application logic, then user interfaces. Evolving architecture can be a pain when you've never done it before, but feature-driven teams can react better to the feedback coming from the customers and reduce risks by, for example, not investing too much on the wrong architecture or the wrong product. Nothing is more inefficient than developing very efficiently a product that nobody wants. Feature-driven cross-functional teams will tend to be generalists, as technically specialized teams will not be able to easily change from one feature to another as demand changes. Feature-driven teams often use user stories as units of work to develop, with every user story describing a feature to be incorporated to the existing product. User stories are supposed to include a description of who wants the feature, what does he want, why (the problem to be solved), and how to test the feature at the end of the iteration. They are frequently handwritten on an index card and posted on the teams' iteration board.

- *Planning game*: In more traditional environments, a project manager plans the whole project, divides work, estimates effort and costs, and then blames everyone for not following the plan and not working hard enough. Agile teams participate as a whole in project planning, as everyone will have valuable information in his part of the project. Estimates are shared and discussed as a way to have more conversations about the product we are building. Teams that share planning are also more committed to delivery dates than those whose delivery date has been set up by someone seen as external to the team. The use of games like planning poker, story points, or workshops to create user story maps is frequent in Agile teams.

- *Co-location*: The benefits of co-locating the cross-functional team together have been widely explained in literature. The time to address the person that could have the answer to your needs drops dramatically, collaboration starts to happen naturally, and osmotic communication takes place. Alistair Cockburn, father of the concept of osmotic communication, says that "information flows into the background hearing of members of the team, so that they pick up relevant information as though by osmosis".[8]

- *Pair programming*: This practice started among developers, but it is gradually being applied by other members of the team. For example, developers and testers are pairing, so code is easier to test. And analysts and coders are pairing so coders better understand what they need to solve, and also produce more readable code. When two people pair, only one computer is used. While one of them is at the keyboard, the other plays the navigator or observer role. Pair programming has proven to produce better code quality, hence reducing the number of bugs and improving performance. It is also a great way of learning and sharing knowledge between team members.

- *Visual management*: Agile teams love to post things on their walls. Iteration state, who is working on what, project progress, impediments, definition of "Done"... even appreciation messages from one team member to another. The Agile team's "Visual War Room" has a lot of influence on team members: it puts some peer pressure on them, while also creating a team culture of what is important for them and what they are striving for. A direct heritage from Lean environments, no software tool has ever matched the subtle power of physical team boards!

- *Agile coach*: Agile companies have found teamwork to be the ultimate competitive advantage. But they've also learned that putting some people together, throwing a project to them, and calling them "team" will not necessarily produce the kind of magic they are searching for. The role of the Agile coach is both teaching Agile practices and coaching the team to make the most out of them. This usually includes coaching individual team members, helping the team solve their conflicts, teaching them to communicate in a constructive way, facilitating meetings, making them trust one another, or showing them ways to remove impediments by themselves.

> "It is teamwork that remains the ultimate competitive advantage, both because it is so powerful and so rare."
>
> –Patrick Lencioni, *The Five Dysfunctions of a Team*

---

[8] Cockburn A (2004) Crystal clear: a human powered methodology for small teams. Addison-Wesley Professional.

• *Retrospectives*: At frequent intervals, the team reflects on what is going well, and how to spread those practices, and what is going wrong, so they find ways to improve it. The behavior of the team is automatically changed in order to implement the improvement plan they have designed, and the appropriate processes and documentation are updated to show these changes.

Agile also has a wide spectrum of technical practices for developers. Agile developers share the ownership of the whole application, so everyone is entitled to modify someone else's code. Tests are written prior to the code, and then only the code needed to pass the tests is written. Once all tests are passing, the code is refactored to make it simpler, smaller, and more efficient. Every piece of finished code is automatically built into the whole application, and alarms stop the development process if the build is broken – again, a direct heritage from Lean environments, where the Jidoka or autonomation principle will stop the whole production line when a problem is detected.

Agile in a Nutshell

Again, trying to summarize Agile seems a Herculean task, but I'll try to give an overall image of how an Agile environment feels like:

It's Monday morning on Agile Enterprise Inc. A new project is launching, so a User Story Mapping workshop has been set up by the Agile Coach. Representatives from the client have come to explain their problem to the team, and the team starts to make questions about the desired behavior of the system they will be building. Groups of features (epics) start to be identified and posted to the wall, and a general skeleton of the application takes form. After several hours, some hundred features have been defined at high level and prioritized by the client, so the coach calls for the workshop to end. A short retrospective of the workshop is conducted to see what can be improved next time and how valuable was the time invested.

On Tuesday the team plans for an iteration of two weeks, and they estimate that the first twelve features can be done by the end of the iteration. An iteration board is designed showing the features to be developed in "pending" state. While the iteration goes on, each feature will be moved to "analysis," "development," "testing," and "done!" to show their progress. The team will make an effort to have
(continued)

as few open features at a time as possible, thus reducing the work in progress and the context switching. This will give the team better concentration and performance, and the overall lead time will also improve.

Every day the team will gather together standing up in front of the board and tell the other team members what they are working at, how much is still to be done, what they will be doing next and what problems and impediments they are facing. The board will be updated, so it will always show the current iteration state, and the team will go back to work. The coach will take note of the impediments and help the team when they find one that blocks a feature: their priority will be always to solve the impediment, and not to abandon the feature in favor of an easier, unblocked but less valuable and less priority item.

Exactly two weeks later, not a day after, a meeting with the client takes place. The team managed to successfully finish ten out of the twelve planned features. Unexpected technical issues were discovered: fortunately enough, we are still on time to re-plan the whole project, as only two weeks have been invested and the knowledge we have right now, after physically working on the code for two weeks, is much higher than the one we had when thinking and designing with pencil and paper.

The ten features or user stories are accepted by the client, but now that he sees and uses the features and knows how they feel, he realizes that some new features will be needed. He also notices that some of the features on the original backlog will not be very valuable, as the current features cover most of the functionality that the non-developed features will provide, so some changes and re-arrangements are made to the feature backlog, and the team plans for a new iteration.

Before starting the new iteration, the Coach calls for an iteration retrospective. The team is happy with their collaboration level and the way they are reporting and managing the project, but they are a bit upset about the technical issues they weren't able to predict. All of them have something to do with an arcane module of their legacy code-base that nobody really knows how it works. So they start thinking about a way to refactor this module and turn it into something more stable, bug-free, and documented. Some capacity of the team will be spared to work on this module and, while this will drop the team's velocity for a couple of iterations, reducing the number of blocked stories and impediments will probably rise the team's throughput later.

Summary

Lean and Agile are frameworks that very often seem counterintuitive. We've usually been educated on Taylor's paradigms of man-hours, carrots and sticks, bosses and subordinates, hyper-specialization, and *Dilbertesque* office environments. While companies have fancy mission statements that state the importance of the customer, the usual fact is that they ignore and abuse them in order to raise their profit, and while the companies often say that their workers are their most important asset, downsizing, offshoring, and institutionalized abuse, harassment, and exploitation are in the order of business.

> "You are not paid to think. A mindless worker is a happy worker. Shut up and do your job!"
>
> —Futurama de-motivational poster

On the other hand, Lean and Agile rest on the foundation of real client focus – maximizing value from the client's perspective, comanagement, teamwork, empowerment, motivation, values, pride... Put it this way, it is normal that many people will say "that will never work", but it is working. It has been working for decades, in fact.

Lean companies are four times as productive as their market's average, their quality is ten times better, and their costs are less than half that of their competitors. These rates skyrocket if we study companies based on knowledge workers, where the best of their field can be 30 or 50 times better than the average, with this number growing even more when the knowledge field gets more complex.

Companies working by the old twentieth-century paradigms face a dramatic decision: if they go on trying to brute-force their business by lowering costs, they will need to fight against the rising economies like China, Korea, Brazil, India, or Russia, where labor costs are cheaper and people usually work for 12 h a day, 6 days a week.

On the other hand, they can embrace Japan's model of efficiency, quality, and continuous improvement, but this is not possible without a committed and aligned workforce.

So the question is, how can we turn our listless and individualized workforce into a Lean-Agile set of true collaborating teams capable of beating the heck out of the market?

This, above all, is the Agile manager's role.

Things to Try

- Visualize your value stream. Find some books or tutorials on the topic, and then start by mapping your whole production process backward with the help of no more than a pencil and a notebook. Start with the deliveries of the goods, then go back step by step until you reach the point where an order from the client was received. Don't trust the people's estimate: measure the time by tracing the orders, receipts, delivery tickets, e-mails, and any other available information. Try to find out how much time was spent really working on the product and how much was wasted in queues, waiting time, handoffs, reworks. . . Identify bottlenecks and design a plan to exploit them.

- List your main sources of waste. Read about Muda, Mura, and Muri as a way to inspire yourself and learn to see waste around. Look carefully at every activity and ask yourself "do we really want to do more of it?" If not, label it as waste and try to reduce it in the future. Try to quantify the cost this activity has in the overall production process. Make everyone join you in this search for waste.

- Start to schedule regular Gemba Walks: go to the place where actual value is created, the workplace, and spend some time wandering around trying to see if help is needed. Also try to physically follow the value stream from side to side and spot hidden sources of waste, bottlenecks, current issues, and possible improvements. Don't use Gemba Walks to interrupt people and ask them about the state of work: only address people if a problem in the system as a whole has been spotted, or if they ask you for your help.

- Use your value stream to start a Kanban board. Gather all ongoing and pending work and represent it on a board with all the Value Stream steps. You can find excellent recommended tutorials on Kanban at the end of this chapter. Note down every step the work takes and start measuring cycle time and lead time. Use your Kanban board to encourage discussion and reflection among teams about current issues, bottlenecks, prioritization schemas, sources of waste, and improvements of the current process.

- Start a visual management program. Organizations are as mature as the information is free to travel across them. If people want to hide information, there is something to be addressed there. Urge everyone to make the information about their projects immediately visible and constantly updated. Reinforce the visual management program with an A3 initiative: urge everyone to design A3 forms for their reports and documents.

- Launch a Kaizen program. You can start by asking everyone to do periodical retrospectives – every 2 or 3 weeks is a good place to start. Ask people to list things that are working well and things that are not. Every retrospective exercise should end with a list of proposed actions – if not, it's just whining!

- Ask your coworkers what problems they face in their daily jobs. If they answer "No problem!" make them realize that "No problem" is a problem, as it hides the path to continuous improvement. Try to ask them what they would need to double productivity with the same resources they have right now.

- For every recurrent problem or error detected, launch a root cause analysis workshop. Try to find the roots of the problem by asking, "Why?" (Toyota is well known for using five why's for every detected problem). Learn about Ishikawa fishbone diagrams, as well as cause-effect diagrams.

- Think of a way to work on smaller work batches more frequently. Try to release something to your client every 2 weeks or so, gather client's feedback, and then replan according to the feedback received. Invite your client to the planning meetings.

- Train your people on Agile and Lean. Then, let them figure out what parts of Agile and Lean they could be using. Don't try to implement the whole set at once – you'll inevitably fail! Start by understanding the core principles and values instead.

- If you work at a software development or IT company, gradually introduce some of the Agile practices described. Find more practices and tools in some of the recommended readings. Even if you are not at a software company, try to introduce some work-in-pairs time every week: you'll be amazed with the results! Remember to rotate the pairs in order to obtain the best results in terms of knowledge sharing.

- Find and join some Lean or Agile practitioners group in your city. If there is not one, join an online group. You'll find interesting communities of practice in Yahoo groups, Google groups, or LinkedIn.

Recommended Readings

Anderson DJ (2010) Kanban – successful evolutionary change for your technology business. Blue Hole Press, Sequim

Beck K (1999) Extreme programming explained: embrace change. Addison-Wesley Professional, Boston

Cockburn A (2006) Agile software development: the cooperative game. Addison-Wesley Professional, Upper Saddle River

Cohn MW (2009) Succeeding with agile: software development using scrum. Addison-Wesley Professional, Upper Saddle River

Dowser J (1999) Embracing defeat: Japan in the wake of World War II. W. W. Norton & Company, New York

Ishikawa K (1991) What is totally quality control? The Japanese way. Productivity Press, Cambridge

Kniberg H, Skarin M (2010) Kanban and Scrum – making the most of both. lulu.com, Raleigh

Liker JK (2003) The Toyota way: 14 management principles from the world's greatest manufacturer. McGraw-Hill, New York

Nonaka I, Takeuchi H (1995) The knowledge-creating company: how Japanese companies create the dynamics of innovation. Oxford University Press, New York

Ohno T (1988) Toyota production system: beyond large-scale production. Productivity Press, Portland

Ohno T (2009) Workplace management. Gemba Press, Mukilteo

Poppendieck M, Poppendieck T (2003) Lean software development: an Agile toolkit. Addison-Wesley Professional, Boston

Poppendieck M, Poppendieck T (2006) Implementing lean software development: from concept to cash. Addison-Wesley Professional, Boston

Poppendieck M, Poppendieck T (2009) Leading lean software development: results are not the point. Addison-Wesley Professional, Boston

Rother M, Shook J (1999) Learning to see: value-stream mapping to create value and eliminate Muda. Lean Enterprise Institute, Cambridge

Shingo S (2007) Kaizen and the art of creative thinking: the scientific thinking mechanism. PCS Inc. and Enna Products Corporation, Vancouver

Shingo S (2009) Fundamental principles of lean manufacturing. PCS Inc. and Enna Products Corporation, Vancouver

Tabb WK (1995) The postwar Japanese system: cultural economy and economic transformation. Oxford University Press, New York

Womack JP, Jones DT (2003) Lean thinking: Banish waste and create wealth in your corporation. Free Press, New York

Womack JP, Jones DT, Roos D (1991) The machine that changed the world: the story of lean production. Harper Perennial, New York

The Agile Manager's Role

Managing an Agile Organization or the Joy of Herding Kittens

3

Managers Versus Self-Organization

Management literature is a profitable and recurrent business. Hundreds, if not thousands, of books have been written on the topic of motivating employees, setting strategies, making decisions, growing the company, and so on, so why do we need new books specially suited for the Agile organization?

For me, the main answer is self-organization.

One of the Agile Manifesto principles reads, "The best architectures, requirements, and designs emerge from self-organizing teams." The topic of self-organization has always been a fuzzy area in Agile: teams are supposed to "self-organize" and go into a hyper-productive frenzy of astonishing products and outstanding innovation. Why self-organization?

Even worse: very often, even when the processes, the tools, the practices, and the artifacts are in place, and even when the team wholeheartedly embraces Agile values and principles, self-organization and hyper-productivity do not happen. Why not?

In their search for hyper-productivity, Agile pioneers from Nonaka-Takeuchi to Poppendieck, Sutherland, or Beck found that teams reaching this kind of state were absolutely not micromanaged or told what to do and how to do it. Instead, these teams had a goal and a purpose, and they collaborated to find the best ways to reach that goal. Of course, some boundaries and constraints such as deadlines, budget, or technology were set up by the organization, but these teams created a sort of "organization within the organization," seeing themselves more as "Team Inc." than a bunch of subordinates waiting for specific orders.

Á. Medinilla, *Agile Management*, DOI 10.1007/978-3-642-28909-5_3,
© Springer-Verlag Berlin Heidelberg 2012

Agile companies are trying to replicate this kind of environment. If you look at them from the Lean perspective, what they are looking for is the kind of empowerment and ownership that a Japanese worker shows when he decides to stop the whole production line because he feels like there is something that could be done better, and he owes that kind of perfection to the company and its customers.

But if the team self-organizes, what is the role of the Agile manager? What if the team decides to do something that the company doesn't like? Even if we embrace self-organization, what if we tell them to self-organize and they stare at us paralyzed with blank faces, as the rabbit looking at the front lights of the truck?

We will learn more on self-organization in later chapters, but for now we will focus on the role of the Agile manager in a self-organizing environment.

Agile's Black Hole

Let's start by accepting that Agile as a whole has always been very team-centric. A sort of reaction against bad management has taken place, and when small self-organizing teams have proven great results, the temptation to say "See? And we did it without management support... All we ask management for is to step out of our path!" is too hard to resist.

So we have books on coaching teams, the Agile coach role, the product owner, the product itself, all sort of Agile processes and frameworks, Agile programming, Agile tools, Agile testing, Agile estimating, Agile planning, Agile retrospectives... It is just a matter of time before we have some book on Agile coffee making. But only a few books have recently come out addressing the topic of Agile management.

Which is dramatic. According to my experience implementing Agile in all kinds of organizations, when the team reaches the boundaries of their own tiny environment and bumps into the enterprise level, everything stops. Nobody knows what to do and how to pull management into the Agile initiative. We have come to a place where some Agile big names have started to question the whole "Agile at the enterprise level" as something that will never happen.

So, from a Lean perspective, we have a huge suboptimization problem. Maybe we have a hyper-productive, self-organizing, motivated, and always improving team of coders and testers. But still the company's lead time can be suffering from bad requirements, long proposal and contract-signing time, inefficient delivery, wrong projects to work at. . . And how can a small team of developers and testers fix that? "It's not our job!" they cry. And then we blame them for not been committed enough. Because the Agile books say that, they, as an Agile team, and their Agile coach with them should be "removing impediments".

Another example: maybe you have a super-duper team of coders doing terrific Agile stuff, but they feel that they should be cross-functional and have some analysts, testers, graphic designers, and platform people join them. Unfortunately, the company processes and structure don't allow that. And thus, the Agile initiative crashes into the strong barrier of the status quo.

When these Agile teams search for help in seminars, conferences, or community groups, they usually find the "Go Change the World" advice – go talk to the manager, form a community of practice, evangelize, train your people, show results – which is good advice and can work. I have seen it. But it is not what usually happens. What usually happens is that some managers will be scared of the self-organization thing, or will think that Agile is a nice thing to put on the company description as long as it doesn't disrupt the way things are usually done there, or maybe just will be uncomfortable with change, and will kill any attempt of Agile traveling out from the team microenvironment.

> "Most organizations that have adopted Agile methods have not taken them very far. As long as Agile initiatives can occur without disrupting the non-Agile organizational container in which they reside, Agile teams are allowed to function as they please within the scope of their own work assignments. But this is only a starting point for larger-scale organizational improvement. In organizations that have pushed the envelope of Agile practice, people are reaching the limits of improvements that can be achieved within existing structures and business processes. They have grown their Agile practice to the point that it has started to scrape the walls of the non-Agile container in which they reside: the conventional organization. Further progress will require us to re-shape the organization"
>
> –Dave Nicolette, *The IT Portfolio as a Form of Waste*

Anyway, What's a Manager?

At the risk of being repetitive: Anyway, what is a manager?

We made a small introduction to the manager versus leader discussion in Chap. 1, and we have also defined "Agile" briefly. In order to describe "Agile management," maybe the "management" part needs to be clarified.

When I ask this question on Agile management seminars, invariably the first answers I get go in the line of "someone who gives orders," "someone who tells people what to do," and "someone who organizes things." Of course, if your definition of manager goes that way, the concept of "self-organization" will be immediately associated with anarchy, chaos, and we-don't-need-no-stinkin'-management-here.

But I feel like these kinds of ideas are more in the line of "boss" than manager. In other words, our minds are still struggling with feudalism and Fordism when addressing the management concept.

For the sake of this book, I ask you to consider the manager as someone responsible for all or some of the following:

- Establish a vision and a mission for the company/area/department.
- Communicate purpose.
- Determine goals in terms of productivity, quality, innovation, etc.
- Align efforts to achieve the proposed goals.
- Design and execute the strategy, meaning the long-term goals for his management area.
- Serve as a bridge or spokesman with investors, management board, and clients.
- Coordinate, synchronize, and mediate among different teams.
- Assign resources and allocate costs.
- Establish and validate rules, constraints, and boundaries: set the appropriate context for teams.
- Organize growth and define structure.
- Hire and fire.
- Determine salary and bonus policies.
- Work at the portfolio level: prioritize projects, define deadlines, decide whether to release or not, etc.
- Improve system as a whole.
- Create, define, and sustain a corporate culture.
- Motivate and give credit to employees.
- Connect people inside the company: establish value networks.
- Establish career paths and help employees to reach their full potential.
- Drive change.

Blame Management, Power Harvesting, Micromanagement, Command and Control, and Other Machiavellic Workplace Sports

If you carefully review the previous list, you will realize that I avoided things like supervising, controlling, measuring, auditing, punishing, or telling people how to do things. It is not by accident.

Unfortunately, if you follow a day in the life of many managers nowadays, you will find that it will be very difficult to connect their usual activities to one of the topics from the previous list. What you will probably observe will be constant phone calls, never-ending e-mail inboxes, meeting after meeting, and short breaks to make sure that everyone is still busy enough.

Some managers are absolutely dedicated to office politics, trying to progress in the corporate hierarchy by forging alliances, making their competitors fall by blaming them for everything that is not going well in the company, or trying to make their tiny empire grow by incorporating more and more resources. In the meanwhile, every time a request arrives, they will handle it to their team with a label that reads "urgent!" even if it changes yesterday's priorities. On an especially bad occasion I observed at a company, all priorities were changed 22 min after the planning meeting ended! These managers very often see themselves as old-style feudal warlords trying to make their fief prosper, and terror is just one more management tool of the set – sometimes their preferred one!

> "The trouble with coercive power is that it only strengthens resistance. And, if successful, its controlling effect lasts only as long as the force is strong. It is not organic. Only persuasion and the consequent voluntary acceptance are organic"
>
> –Robert K. Greenleaf, *Servant Leadership*

Other managers are so into the Taylor model of "thinking managers and mindless labor" that they feel the urge to establish control mechanisms to make sure that everyone is doing exactly what they have been told and reaching their daily production quota. Performance reviews are filled regularly to reward top performers and punish low performers, a carrot-and-stick mechanism based both on if-then rewards, and the fear of being punished or even fired. They also feel like they are the ones who should diagnose every situation, decide what to do and how to do it, and then give precise instructions to every single person so they execute their will exactly. The word "micromanagement" was coined to depict such managers.

This kind of mechanism can work on a car production line, where everyone is supposed to do the same job day after day until the day they retire – and still it has been proven to be less efficient and productive than the Japanese way of managing, as we explained when we talked about the NUMMI plant experiment. But try to think of a software company: nobody is ever doing the same code that he did yesterday! The environment is changing fast, technology is always evolving constantly, and requirements are so fuzzy that you need a whole squad of business analysts to try to transform them into something actually workable at. I remember a situation where a particularly incompetent project manager was asking a team to give an estimation of time and money to build "a web." That was more or less their whole requirements specification document and project kickoff!

Another problem with command-and-control style of management is that it rarely produces a committed, engaged, and proactive workforce – people just lay around waiting for someone to tell them what to work at next. In a company I was coaching at, everyone was so used to a command and control that when I asked a team what they would do if their manager didn't show up one morning, they sincerely replied "Oh, that's great news, we get a day off!" Their manager, instead of seeing this as a problem, was so proud of himself: he was absolutely essential for the company! And, of course, what he wouldn't tell is that he was so scared that if the team found a way to actually know what to do without him being there to tell them, what would be his contribution to the system? He would be expendable!

Command-and-control and punish-reward mechanisms are great when you want conformance to process or you need people to exactly execute a repetitive and algorithmic task. But when you want engagement, innovation, creativity, and the ability to react in complex environments, another kind of approach is needed.

You have to remember that, from a Lean perspective, all management is waste – especially the kinds I have been describing in the last paragraphs. That means that if we want to be Lean and strive for improvement, we should have as few managers as possible.

But not less.

The War Against Evil Management: Software Anarcho-Syndicalism

Taylorism has had a terrible effect on the software industry. Huge firms have been built to provide IT services to a technology-dependent world that still doesn't really understand the nature of those services. From the typical client perspective, there is no difference between one Java programmer and another, so coders are treated by their employers as commodities: expendable resources that have no distinctive value on their own. Products have been quantified in terms of man-hours; deadlines and schedules have been arbitrarily set by people who don't understand technology and whose main drivers are budget and costs, and so projects have been launched with a fixed price, fixed delivery date, fixed functionality set, and no room for software's inherent uncertainty or complexity.

The result has been poor quality. When you have to deliver something on Friday and you clearly see that you are not going to make it, you panic. And then the trick of the trade is to code for 16 h a day (which introduces more bugs), and drop documentation, testing, or any kind of quality assurance (which again lowers code quality).

The low quality of code produces bugs, trouble reports, system failures and also makes it more difficult to extend the existing code base. So coders are condemned to a living hell of impossible deadlines, crappy products that they abhor, and constant interruptions coming from their previous projects, in a sort of punishment for their quality sins. And who do they blame for all this evil? Managers, of course. After all, it wasn't them who pushed the deadline beyond the limits of reason.

In a sort of counterreaction movement, many oppressed employees living in these sick environments started to organize themselves in Internet forums, professional conventions, or local groups. Some of these people bumped into the Agile Manifesto, and what they read was "No More Processes, No More Documents, No More Contracts, No More Planning – Just plain coding and joy." They seem to have forgotten to read the "while there is value on these items" part.

Let's face it and be honest about it: many fugitives from the cubicle farms have seen Agile as a lifesaver in the war between bad managers and good developers. I have had literally hundreds of them at my seminars, claiming that every single evil that the organization is suffering comes from management. Some of them even claim that the whole organization, including marketing, sales, finances, human resources, legal, and, above all, management, is not important at all – what is *really* important is the beauty and quality of code!

It is no surprise to see that, year after year, one of the most well-known surveys on Agile adoption, Version One's "State of Agile" yearly survey, constantly lists organizational culture, resistance to change, and lack of management support as some of the most important barriers to Agile adoption.

When you start this line of reasoning, it is easy to end up demanding the end of company structures as we know them and the rise of a new kind of management-less anarchy led by the purpose of beautiful code – Software Anarchy! In fact, doesn't the Manifesto itself talk about self-organization?

For these management skeptics, any kind of organization will come in the form of communities of practice, or maybe coding cells of collaboration and mutual interest in order to perform big projects – like trade unions. That is why I use the term "Software Anarcho-Syndicalism" to – with all due respect – refer to their idea.

As an Agile manager, you have to be aware that, in all probability, this kind of reasoning will be around you sometimes. So what are you going to do? Act as a feudal lord and bash any kind of opposition? Institutionalize a political police?

Yup, but...

It is both sad and surprising that the revolutionary field of information technology, one of the current pillars for progress and innovation, is producing this kind of anachronistic argumentations. Maybe it is that we, knowledge workers, also demand the opportunity to have our social revolution and step back from the perils of savage Taylorism. But if this is the case, I feel like there are better ways to find more humane and successful work environments than to ban all management.

The truth is that pure anarchy is still to be proven. Some radical experiments have taken place with good results in a handful of places, but all of them still have some kind of managerial structure. Some of them will be studied in the chapter about self-organization.

Another truth you must understand is that self-organization is not the same as self-management. Self-management means that the team can decide on what product to build, which markets to enter, which clients to approach, or when to spin off a company. That can be true for a start-up, a self-organizing, and self-managed group of people who engage in a risky endeavor to bootstrap a company from scratch. But in most teams, self-management is not an existing condition.

Even if teams were capable of some kind of self-management, for instance, in the start-up team, the need for coordination and management will also rise as the structure grows. It is easy to self-manage for a group of five but not so easy for 200 people. When the company gets bigger, the solution is not to create bigger teams, as they tend to collapse when the headcount goes over the 10–12 people mark, as we will discuss in the chapter about Agile structures. The Agile solution is to create more teams, and then the need to coordinate and align them with a common purpose while looking at the system as a whole appears. In other words, someone has to lead the path, keep the sheep together, and protect them from wolves.

In fact, if you take a look at Software Anarcho-Syndicalism preachers, you will see that most of them work on their own, or maybe in tiny shop-like companies of no more than five or ten people. There is a reason for that: manager-less environments haven't been proven on bigger companies. Please understand that I'm absolutely fine with that: I, myself, have worked for huge companies whose employees were counted by the thousands, and also as a freelancer, and I have found myself more comfortable working on my own. But I don't wake up at ten in the morning, sip a coffee in my pajamas while answering e-mail, and then say "Oh, who needs any process and hierarchy for this? Let's go preach for process-less environments to people in the corporate world…."

So yes, except for tiny shop-like companies, which are absolutely OK, there will be a need for managers – for Agile managers.

Lean Management

Let's see it from this other perspective: if what we are seeking is for Leaner companies, Lean being one of the origins of Agile, why don't we look at Lean management?

As I explained when talking about the NUMMI experiment, and also when Konosuke Matsushita was quoted in Chap. 1, the main difference between western-like management and the Japanese concept of managers is that western managers want to tell people what to do, while eastern-like managers have codesigned with the workforce a system that will let everyone know what they are supposed to work at next, without the need for a manager to tell them so. Managers are then available to work at the system as a whole and support their people when they have any kind of impediment, teaching them how to better perform their job, and making them reach their full potential.

In fact, in many Japanese factories, you only get promoted once you've reached a deep knowledge of your current job, and you are considered to provide more value to the company teaching others how to perform it better than just doing your job very well. The principle of "long-term thinking" applies here: when you promote your best worker, you lose him as a productive unit in the short term. But in the long term, everyone will get better at their job, as this person will be available to teach and coach them, and the combined rise of productivity and quality will outperform the former individual contribution of this person.

But in software companies, we usually have a problem you rarely see at manufacturing plants: software developers often know more about their craft than their managers! So if we take the teaching out of the Lean management concept, what do we have left?

Well, there is the "servant leader" part of the equation. Managers are available to serve the teams, helping them remove corporate impediments, providing the needed resources, discussing the current boundaries and constraints, and coordinating with other teams in order to make the whole system run smoothly. Lean managers will also provide a long-term view, a core Lean principle, while the teams, because of their inherent nature, will tend to focus on short-term deliveries.

There is also the problem solving. While everyone is busy at this week's project, the Lean manager will take his time to wander around helping and looking for unspotted bottlenecks, current problems, and feasible improvements – remember the Genchi Genbutsu/Gemba Kaizen practices! But please understand that, in Lean at its best, the Lean manager will not be the one responsible for fixing problems, but for making sure that there is a working problem-solving process that makes everyone care about improving the system on a daily basis.

> "Everybody, everyday solving problems, that's the only answer to the Pareto dilemma. You've got to visualize two flows in the plant. One: the product flow[. . .]. Two: the problem flow to the person who finally solves the problem. [. . .] you shouldn't funnel all problems to your key technical people. You should protect them to work on the really difficult issues. What you have to organize is the problem solving in the line!"
>
> –Michael and Freddy Balle, *The Lean Manager: A Novel of Lean Transformation*

Agile Management

At the beginning of this chapter, we discussed several tasks and duties for managers, and then we dedicated several pages to discuss things that shouldn't define the manager's role. We've even described the Lean management concept, but what about Agile management?

Well, the fact is that only recently the role of management in Agile has been seriously discussed in literature, and even field experience reports from companies doing Agile for a long time are generally restricted to the practices and processes of the team. The good side of this situation is that I am more or less free to define what is an Agile manager for me!

So I'll give you my own view, the one I use when helping companies to implement Agile at a corporate level: an Agile manager is, above all, a manager. Only that he has to perform his job in an Agile environment. That means he has to deal with self-organizing teams of knowledge workers creating complex products in an iterative and incremental approach, which calls for special structures, motivation schemes, client relationships, workload management styles, and corporate culture.

According to this definition, and trying to summarize the manager's role discussed in this chapter, the Agile manager would be responsible and accountable for:

• Motivating and developing Agile teams
• Managing self-organizing teams and aligning their efforts with the purpose and goals of the company
• Creating an Agile structure
• Managing workload (the project portfolio) and capacity in an Agile way
• Building an Agile corporate culture and driving change
While he would also be responsible for continuously improving the whole system, he would not be the only one involved in that task, as the team and their coach will have an important and constant role identifying impediments and solving problems, so I have left the Kaizen management area aside – maybe as a subject for next books.

We will dedicate the following chapters to each of these Agile management areas.

The Agile Leader

As we explained in Chap. 1, there is a difference between being a manager and being a leader. You can be just an Agile manager, which means you will be managing on an Agile environment, and that is fine. In fact, it is difficult enough! If that is your goal, I expect that the contents of this book will help you get started – and hopefully drive you some miles into the path.

But becoming an Agile leader means that you will represent the Agile concept to your people. You must understand and embrace Agile values and principles, being the first to evangelize, teach, implement, and defend them. If that is your will, congratulations! You've chosen a difficult path reserved only for the finest and the bravest. But in order to become an Agile leader, coach, and mentor, you'll need to develop yourself far beyond the contents of this book.

Anyway, this book can give you a solid foundation to become an Agile leader. In order to gain that status, you must start by committing yourself to helping and serving others, not to make them follow you. Agile leaders renounce the hierarchical view of the organization and, instead, demonstrate a sense of community and shared management.

Both Agile managers and leaders need to quit the command-and-control behaviors and the need to impose their own criteria and values through the use of coercive power. But Agile leaders will also listen and demonstrate empathy with those working with them – not for them. Agile leaders will constantly communicate a vision and a purpose that will be created by everyone in the company, not just the management board, and they will constantly show a full commitment to the improvement and development of individuals, the company, and the community.

Agile leaders will inspire everyone in the darkest hours and remain as the last standing man when it comes to defending an Agile view of the organization. They will make sure that the Agile implementation process goes on and constantly strengthen the common vision by continuous follow-up.

> "People want to sign on. They want to be enrolled. Nobody listening to the president that day had the reaction 'Oh damn, now I have to do stuff for my country'. On the contrary, they were delighted. The emergence of a leader is a source of satisfaction and completion for all. People want to be led toward a vision that is consistent with reality and their present assessment of the culture. When an organization is in drift and then suddenly everyone is aware that a hand has taking the

helm, the sense of relief is palpable. The fact that people want to be led is what makes leadership possible at all."

–Tom de Marco, *Slack: Getting Past Burnout, Busywork, and the Myth of Total Efficiency*

Things to Try

- For every individual and team you are managing, schedule a meeting and ask them to bring a list of things you could be doing to help them better perform their work. Try to identify common areas, and use them as a foundation to define your role as a servant leader. Follow up these meetings with other meetings where you ask them to help you define the role of a manager in the forthcoming Agile organization: what would they expect an Agile manager to be?

- Start a list with every single command or assignment you give to your people. For each of them, try to think on a system that will automatically route these assignments to the appropriate person, maybe with the help of the team itself. If you don't trust them to do this work correctly, teach them to do so and ask them to devise a visual tool that lets you see at any given moment who is doing what, so you can detect and correct mistakes. When a mistake has been made on a job assignment, don't just fix it. Gather the team and ask them why did they make that decision. If you still think that it is a mistake, explain to them why and ask them to implement a rule, process, or change into the system that will prevent this problem happening again. As the system gets perfected, you'll need less time to assign work and review the work-assignment process: use that time to work at the Agile manager's job areas described in this book.

- Create a list with the areas where you have decision power and the ones that the team can decide on. Try to spot some areas that you can move from the first list to the second. The chapter on self-organization can help you find ways to do so.

- Place a feedback board near your desk where everyone can post concerns about your management style and also share how are you helping them (or not).

- Progressively make your team participate in management decisions, first as a set of consultants while you remain as the one taking the final decision, and gradually moving to a co-management style of decision making.

- Treat any change on priorities or need to "hit-and-run" your team with micromanagement orders as a national emergency. File an A3 report on it and try to trace the roots of the problem. Never assume that "these things will always happen" or "this is normal stuff," and try to find ways to prevent these issues showing up again.

- Increase your knowledge on the technical areas of the people you are managing. Don't assume that you can manage software developers without minimally understanding the nature of the systems they are building. Even a minimal true interest in the technology, architecture, or tools that your people are using will be seen by them as a show of respect and concern.

- Engage in an Agile foundations training seminar with your people. Use that opportunity as a chance to discuss with them how to manage the organization with the mediation and facilitation of a professional – and neutral – Agile coach.

Recommended Readings

Appelo J (2011) Management 3.0: leading Agile developers, developing Agile leaders. Addison-Wesley Professional, Upper Saddle River

Balle M, Balle F (2009) The lean manager: a novel of lean transformation. Lean Enterprise Institute, Cambridge, MA

De Marco T (2002) Slack: getting past burnout, busywork, and the myth of total efficiency. Broadway, New York

De Marco T, Lister T (1999) PeopleWare: productive projects and teams. Dorset House, New York

Greenleaf RK (2002) Servant leadership: a journey into the nature of legitimate power and greatness. Paulist Press, New York

Kotter JP (1997) Matsushita leadership. Free Press, New York

Liker J, Convis GL (2011) The Toyota way to lean leadership: achieving and sustaining excellence through leadership development. McGraw-Hill, New York

Spolsky J (2004) Joel on software. Apress, New York

Spolsky J (2008) More Joel on Software. Apress, New York

Part II

Agile Management

Motivating the Agile Workforce

4

From the Happiness of Survival to the Meaning of Life

Why Motivation Is Essential for Knowledge Workers: Medinilla's Principle of Motivation

The principles behind the Agile Manifesto include "build projects around *motivated individuals*. Give them the environment and support they need, and trust them to get the job done." But why is motivation so important? Wouldn't it be enough to make sure that everyone does his part of the job and delivers on time, no matter how grumpy or listless they are?

Not in an Agile environment, of course. But again, why? Is it because motivated employees are easier to manage? Is it because we, as a company, get listed in the "best places to work at" articles and have better chances to hire talent? Or maybe because human resources want to have better motivation indexes in surveys every year, just to show everyone how good they are doing?

Well all these effects (better places to work at, better talent, better survey results, more manageable workforce) are desirable consequences of investing in motivation. And you could find even more important reasons, like more quality-oriented, creative, and productive employees.

But in my seminars, I always use a principle to show the importance of motivation. I can't remember if I saw it somewhere else: I swear I feel like I invented it, but it has happened before that I read something and later on remembered it as my own idea – sorry, I'm a human!

Anyway, I'll try to call it "Medinilla's principle of motivation" and see if it sticks. It goes something like this:

Á. Medinilla, *Agile Management*, DOI 10.1007/978-3-642-28909-5_4,
© Springer-Verlag Berlin Heidelberg 2012

"Every great product ever created that made a huge difference in the market was created by a highly motivated individual or team. As a corollary, never in history, at no place on earth, a de-motivated individual or workforce gave birth to a great product"

–Medinilla's principle of motivation

Sometimes, when I enunciate the principle, someone raises his hand and says, "Pyramids! Pyramids are a great product that was created by a very de-motivated workforce."

But of course they weren't. Pyramids are a great product that was created by a highly motivated team of architects, engineers, priests, and pharaohs. The crew pushing stones around were no more than machinery: expendable resources and commodities. When some of them died, you just threw away his carcass and replaced him with the first slave coming out of the cage. And we are not talking about the motivation of machinery here.

"Management is nothing more than motivating other people."

–Lee Iacocca

So motivation is essentially dependent on two factors:

- You care about creating great products or providing outstanding service.
- You understand that software developers are not commodities, and the right professional can make a huge difference.

If you feel like you can survive providing crappy products and it doesn't matter if turnover rates are crazy, then why do you care about Agile? Seriously, implementing Agile is not easy, and you are investing a lot of time and effort on something that is not suited for your needs.

But in case you agree on both premises, let's try to understand better where motivation comes from...

The Evolution of Motivation

As we showed in Chap. 1, the concept of management has transformed during the ages from a hierarchical feudal-style structure of lords and vassals to a hierarchical structure of thinking managers and working labor and then to a set of practices, processes, frameworks, and tools to be implemented. In the last few decades, we are seeing the dawn of a new transformation of management based on collaboration, empowerment, self-organization, and continuous improvement: Agile management.

The same happens when we study the concept of human motivation. In the beginning, the main source of motivation was primal: in a very reptilian scheme of things, the universe was divided into four categories – things to eat, things to flee from, things to have sex with, and stones. The main source of motivation, if not the only one, was to stay alive and have offspring. In a world of nomadic hunter-gatherers, you had to invest all your energies in finding food and protecting yourself and your children from predators and other tribes. If you were not fighting or hunting, you just tried to stay quiet and save your energy until the next food quest.

Only when these primal necessities were satisfied could the human being start looking for other sources of motivation, like friendship and social status – above the basic tribal sense of common survival – or even the transcendent need to express himself and leave a legacy behind, something that would prove he had lived and made a difference. This last need or motivation source is possibly what led the first artists to paint their lives on the walls of a cave, and the same factor that led to the construction of the pyramids or the sculpting of Michelangelo's David.

You are probably familiar with this structure of motivation under the name of Maslow's pyramid. Interestingly enough, Maslow's pyramid, which explains that top levels of motivation like self-actualization or self-esteem can only be fulfilled if the low levels of physiological needs or personal safety are covered, was not proposed until as late as 1943!

Previous to Maslow, employers would not worry much about the motivation of their employees: they got paid, so they could afford a roof above their heads and some food for their families, what else should they worry about? But Taylor and Ford changed that dramatically. Ford started paying their workers twice the average wage, which had two very important effects: first, it was very difficult for their workers to quit their job, as they wouldn't find anyone paying that much elsewhere. This was a wise way of protecting the investment that the employer was making training the employees. But on a second effect, workers had enough money to satisfy their physiological and safety needs and some spare money they could start spending in things that, until then, remained as a privileged luxury for a tiny elite. And so, these workers started buying cars, automated laundry machines, radios, etc. The consumer society was born at the same time as the mass production era.

This was not an unintentional move by Ford. It was a well-devised plan of motivation by external incentives. Motivation 2.0, a step beyond the 1.0 "survival motivation," was born.

At the beginning of the twentieth century, several articles were published on on–the-job training of the workforce, some of them addressing the topic of motivation and generally associating it to economic bonuses – carrots and sticks. As pointed out earlier, it was as late as in the 1940s and 1950s that psychologists started to wonder about the sources and nature of motivation in humans. Maslow proposed his hierarchy of needs,[1] and B.F. Skinner, considered the father of behaviorism, published his first works on personal happiness and satisfying work.[2] As explained in Chap. 1, these studies coincided with the birth and rise of a new species: knowledge workers, whose motivation schemes seemed to be different from those of the typical production line workers.

But it was by 1960 that the two proposals that influenced most of the works on motivation performed later came up.

First, Frederick Herzberg proposed the two-factor theory,[3] distinguishing between extrinsic motivation – you are motivated by something coming from the outside in the form of rewards – and intrinsic motivation – your motivation comes from the inside, in the form of doing what you enjoy, getting better at it, and being proud of your work.

Herzberg's model acted upon Maslow's hierarchy, adding a new dimension in which two different sets of characteristics added job satisfaction or dissatisfaction at the same time, meaning that both operate independently: at any given moment, you can have things that make your job pleasant and things that make your job unpleasant. An increase in any one of the two sets does not mean an immediate decrease on the other. Herzberg also distinguished between motivators, things that will create motivation if present, and hygiene factors, things that will not create motivation on their own but will de-motivate if not present. It is interesting to notice that most of his theories were based on interviews with knowledge workers, especially engineers and accountants.

---

[1] Maslow AH (1943) A theory of human motivation. Psychol Rev 50(4):370–396.

[2] Skinner BF (1953) Science and human behavior. Free Press.

[3] Herzberg F, Mausner B, Snyderman BB (1959) The motivation to work. Wiley.

At the same time, Douglas McGregor, from the MIT, proposed a set of contrasting theories about human behavior in the workplace that he named Theory X and Theory Y.[4]

Essentially, Theory X states that workers are lazy, listless, self-concerned, work only for the money, and will only perform properly if economically incentivized and constantly supervised. McGregor states that this theory is valid in some production-line-like businesses but has been proved invalid in modern workplaces, as the use of coercive power and micromanagement tend to de-motivate the knowledge-based workforce, which inevitably leads to poorer results in terms of productivity and creativity.

On the other hand, Theory Y proposals assume a higher condition of the human being and accept that employees can be self-motivating and self-controlling. It even proposes that employees can enjoy their work, thus being able to better use their talent for creative problem solving. Theory Y calls for managers to create more collaborative work environments, minimizing the difference between managers and workers and helping the latter to reach their full potential. This latter set of theories are considered by some as an application of the humanistic school of psychology or, as Maslow called it, "Third Force psychology" – the first two forces being Freud's psychoanalysis and Skinner's behaviorism.

In the 1970s, Mihály Csíkszentmihályi conducted several experiments and interviews to describe the phenomenon of flow, a mental state of high concentration and focused motivation.[5] For flow to happen, a clear goal that makes the person use his/her skills at a high level and represents a challenge is needed, as a low-skilled or too easy task will not motivate enough to get into flow state. According to his research, flow also needs concentration, interruption-free environments, direct and immediate feedback, and a sense of ownership and control over the way the task is to be performed. He also states that the task should be intrinsically rewarding.

> "Success is not the key to happiness. Happiness is the key to success. If you love what you are doing, you will be successful."
>
> –Albert Schweitzer, Nobel Peace Prize 1952

---

[4] McGregor D (1960) The human side of the enterprise. McGraw Hill.

[5] Csikszentmihalyi M (1975) Beyond boredom and anxiety: experiencing flow in work and play. Jossey-Bass.

Also in the 1970s–1980s, *self-determination theory or SDT* was founded by Edward L. Deci and Richard Ryan as a set of theories on human motivation that gained special relevance since the beginning of the twenty-first century, when the research on intrinsic motivation started to grow. SDT proposes that there is an inherent growth tendency in all human beings, and there are three basic innate needs that allow this growth, which are competence, relatedness, and autonomy.[6] Deci and Ryan also conducted several researches on the pernicious effects of external rewards on motivation.

By year 2002, Steven Reiss proposed his 16 forces theory,[7] where he listed a set of 16 basic desires that guide human behavior:

- Acceptance, the need for approval
- Curiosity, the need to learn
- Eating, the need for food
- Family, the need to raise children
- Honor, the need to be loyal to the traditional values of one's clan/ethnic group
- Idealism, the need for social justice
- Independence, the need for individuality
- Order, the need for organized, stable, predictable environments
- Physical activity, the need for exercise
- Power, the need for influence of will
- Romance, the need for sex
- Saving, the need to collect
- Social contact, the need for friends (peer relationships)
- Status, the need for social standing/importance
- Tranquility, the need to be safe
- Vengeance, the need to strike back/to win

In 2009, author Dan H. Pink published *Drive*, a very popular book that has been widely accepted into the Agile body of knowledge.[8] In this book, Pink uses the open-source software movement as a paradigm of his thesis: money-based motivation is an archaic concept, and we must accept that

---

[6] Deci EL, Ryan R (2002). Handbook of self-determination research. University of Rochester Press.

[7] Reiss S (2002) Who am I? The 16 basic desires that motivate our actions and define our personalities. Berkley Trade.

[8] Pink DH (2009) Drive: the surprising truth about what motivates us. Riverhead Hardcover.

knowledge workers are intrinsically motivated by three main forces: autonomy, the need to be self-directed; mastery, the urge to get better at the things we do; and purpose, or the need to feel that we contribute to a greater mission. This is closely related to SDT theory, as you can see, and Pink also uses the SDT experiments as examples of the pernicious effects of money as a motivator for knowledge workers.

Finally, in his 2011 book, *Management 3.0,*[9] Jurgen Appelo synthesizes the work of Reiss, Pink, and other researchers and proposes a set of ten basic desires at the workplace, removing those not applicable like vengeance, sex, or eating – although many companies have motivated their employees with free snacks, beverages, or even lunch menus at the office, and vengeance understood as the urge to strike competitors could also be proposed as a motivator and a company identity factor (us against them). But motivating employees with romance is still illegal in most countries, in case you wonder.

I have gone a step further and reduced the set to five main areas:

- *Security* or hygiene factors, including enough money to have a house, food, clothing, a family, health care, education, and some job stability

- *Self-organization*, the need to have some decision power and some autonomy while pursuing the goals set for you so you can decide how to perform your job and feel some independence

- *Learning*, or the urge to grow your competence, get better at what you do, satisfy your curiosity, and fulfill your need to progress

- *Vision*, the need to feel that you are contributing to a higher, honorable purpose that you can be proud of and you behave according to noble values

- *Networking*, or the need to feel connected and related to other human beings who accept you, belong to a community, and grow your status in it

All these concepts (Maslow's pyramid, two-factor theory, Theory Y, flow, 16 forces, Pink's model, Appelo's synthesis, or even my own view of five areas) conform to Agile's Motivation 3.0 theory, where money is not the main motivator, but a hygiene factor, and workers want to be proud of their work and enjoy it through self-organization, learning, vision, and connecting to others.

---

[9] Appelo J (2011) Management 3.0: leading Agile developers, developing Agile leaders. Addison-Wesley Professional.

Motivation, Fear, Happiness

Before we enter each of the five areas, let's take a look at both ends of the motivation line.

At one end, the lesser one, we have the opposite of motivation, which is not de-motivation. De-motivation is a mere absence of motivation. But if you go even further, what you will find is fear.

There is no chance of motivation if there is fear around. Companies and individuals using fear as a motivator have absolutely lost the point on how to motivate knowledge workers. Maybe fear is useful when motivating a squad of soldiers who must charge against a machine gun nest: if they fear their sergeant enough, they will know that if they don't follow orders, he will put a bullet in their heads immediately, while with the nest they still hold some chance of survival.

But when we are talking about problem solving, creative thinking, and even the most rudimentary cognitive skills, fear is a mind killer.

> "I must not fear.
> Fear is the mind-killer.
> Fear is the little-death that brings total obliteration.
> I will face my fear.
> I will permit it to pass over me and through me.
> And when it has gone past I will turn the inner eye to see its path.
> Where the fear has gone there will be nothing.
> Only I will remain."
>
> –Bene Gesserit litany against fear – Frank Herbert, *Dune*

People in fear will not take risks. That's why most of the people don't quit jobs they hate to pursue their dreams: they are so scared to lose their house, their family, or even the respect of their colleagues. Sometimes even the fear of uncertainty, not knowing what is going to happen, is enough to keep people from trying.

> "*Roy Batty*: Quite an experience to live in fear, isn't it? That's what it is to be a slave."
>
> –Ridley Scott, *Blade Runner*, Warner Bros.

On the other end of motivation, we have happiness – not as an instant, ephemeral feeling of joy, but as a general feeling of satisfaction and well-being with your current situation. It has been demonstrated by positive psychologists (Mihaly Csikszentmihalyi being one of the fathers of the concept) that when you study middle-class workers, several extrinsic factors like money, education, or even a higher IQ have little effect on personal happiness and job satisfaction, while the presence of intrinsic motivation factors (self-organization, learning, vision, networking), cultivating mindfulness through meditation, actively pursuing flow at work, or developing one's strengths and virtues can have a very significant effect.

According to many, including myself, happiness is in great measure a personal commitment. To be happy, the first thing you must do is decide to be happy, as happiness is not something that others can provide but something you must cultivate yourself. It requires both courage and deliberate practice.

> "Happiness is the meaning and the purpose of life, the whole aim and end of human existence', 'Happiness depends upon ourselves"
>
> —Aristotle
>
> "We take greater pains to persuade others we are happy than in trying to think so ourselves."
>
> —Confucius
>
> "You only have reasons to be happy and thankful"
>
> —Siddhartha Gautama Buddha
>
> "Most folks are about as happy as they make up their minds to be"
>
> —Abraham Lincoln
>
> "I am determined to be cheerful and happy in whatever situation I may find myself. For I have learned that the greater part of our misery or unhappiness is determined not by our circumstance but by our disposition."
>
> —Martha Washington

So, as we see, another important effect of motivation in the workplace is to increase the happiness of everyone. Not bad. In fact, many Agile companies have implemented a "happiness index," asking everyone

periodically how happy they are, as the main key performance indicator.[10]
Any decrease in the happiness index is treated as an emergency, and this has
shown beneficial effects on productivity, quality, and customer satisfaction.

Money and Motivation

In his 2009 book, *Drive*, Dan H. Pink mentions a series of experiments
conducted in several universities to measure the effect of economic
incentives on personal performance. The results consistently showed
over and over that, for manual, repetitive, algorithmic-like tasks, money
rewards worked as expected: the bigger the reward, the better the performance. But when any cognitive skills, even rudimentary, were involved
in the experiment, money rewards worked the other way round: small to
medium rewards made no difference, but big rewards made performance
worsen.

Yes, you've read right: people offered a big reward if they reached a
given goal had the worst performance and results of all experiments.
Spooky, right?

This is not what Taylor-style economists would predict. They would say
that if you want workers to perform better, you have to promise money
rewards and bonuses. In fact, the classical pioneers of economics like Adam
Smith linked economy and psychology when studying the dynamics of
microeconomics.[11] But neoclassical economists at the beginning of the
twentieth century abandoned those ideas in favor of a rational conception
of economics, where all behaviors were predictable by equations.

Well, these experiments proved that human behavior is not always
rational or driven by economic efficiency parameters. A new field of
study, behavioral economics, is using human behavior and emotions to
explain inefficient and nonrational phenomena, like stock market bubbles.

So the fact is this: money is a motivation factor only as long as it covers
the most basic needs. Once you feel like you have an income level similar to
the one of your friends, the people that surround you, your neighbors, or

---

[10] I believe that Henrik Kniberg is the father of the Agile-related concept, although you
can trace back to 1972 the use of "Gross National Happiness" by Buthan's King Jigme
Singye Wangchuck, as a better and more holistic quality-of-life and well-being index
than Gross National Product.

[11] Smith A (1759) The theory of moral sentiments. A. Millar.

your university peers, an increase in income will not produce a significant increase in motivation or general happiness.

2002's Nobel Prize winner in Economic Sciences, Daniel Kahneman, puts it this way:

> "Surveys in many countries conducted over decades indicate that, on average, reported global judgments of life satisfaction or happiness have not changed much over the last four decades, in spite of large increases in real income per capita. While reported life satisfaction and household income are positively correlated in a cross-section of people at a given time, increases in income have been found to have mainly a transitory effect on individuals' reported life satisfaction. [. . .] When people consider the impact of any single factor on their well-being –not only income– they are prone to exaggerate its importance; we refer to this tendency as the focusing illusion. [. . .] These findings suggest that the standard survey questions by which subjective well-being is measured (mainly by asking respondents for a global judgment about their satisfaction or happiness with their life as a whole) may induce a form of focusing illusion, by drawing people's attention to their relative standing in the distribution of material well-being. More importantly, the focusing illusion may be a source of error in significant decisions that people make."
>
> –Daniel Kahneman[12]

Of course, in terms of the two-factor theory, money is a hygiene factor. If workers are not paid enough, they will not be motivated no matter how much you invest on self-organization, learning, vision, or networking. Even contributors to open-source projects, who are not paid for it, will not be motivated if they don't have an alternative source of funding that covers their basic needs. So you must pay them enough to get money out of the motivation equation, but never forget the importance of it. Include here any benefits as health care, holidays, or even family-work balance.

An interesting conclusion of these findings is this: bonus schemes don't work the way you would expect in a knowledge-based business. That means

---

[12] Kahneman D et al. (2006) Would you be happier if you were richer? A focusing illusion. Science 312:1908–1910.

that the higher the bonuses, the worse the overall performance. One explanation is that people will be more concerned about their individual bonus than the global functioning of the enterprise, which leads to a suboptimization. Another explanation could be that when choosing between two possible courses of action, one of them leading to improvement and the other one making you more eligible for a bonus, people will tend to choose the latter.

The truth is that most bonus schemes I have found as a consultant for companies are seriously flawed, if not totally broken. People with a 20% variable salary will expect to receive it by the end of the year, and if you don't award them with it, they will feel you are stealing from them: they become bonus addicted. It's very usual for managers I have met to arbitrarily set a goal achievement percentage of 80–90% because less than 80% will upset workers, while more than 90% will seem suspicious from the management board or human resources' point of view. Hence, the whole bonus scheme is not actually enforcing any kind of behavior!

On the other hand, setting individual goals tied to general enterprise performance is a dangerous sport, if not an impossible one. When individual employees see that their bonus is linked to the companies' earnings or client churn rate, they don't know how to relate their daily tasks to these results, so they just do the best they can. By the end of the year, if they have worked hard but the country's economy hasn't been good and profit has lowered, they won't receive their bonus and they will feel like they've been scammed. Of course, as any Lean or complex systems expert will tell you, the way to optimize general performance is not to optimize every single individual contribution to the system, as this will again lead to suboptimization.

So my advice to all the managers who have asked me for an Agile way of setting economic incentives and bonus is this: you are asking a flawed question! Drop the whole bonus scheme. People should be paid enough so they don't care about bonuses, but if bonuses are available, they will be attracted by them no matter how high their salary is, and their behavior will be inefficient in terms of an Agile organization. Get that 20% variable salary and, next year, make it a fixed increase in salary while getting rid of the whole thing.

Bonuses are evil. You can quote me.

Consider Netflix, the 24-million-user media distribution company, and their salary policy: they know that one outstanding employee gets more done and costs less than two just-adequate employees, so their salary strategy is to pay top of the market. That means that if the employee is aware of his market value, meaning how much someone with his skills and experience is being paid for his kind of work, and knows that he would not be making more money elsewhere, then Netflix has moved money out of the motivation equation. It also means that there are no annual rises as long as your market value remains the same. There is no centrally administered "rise pool," so salaries are not a zero-sum game where some employees having rises means that other employees are not able to get them. Even more: rises are not dependent on Netflix success, so even in a bad year, Netflix will pay top of the market to their employees because if they don't do so, they will lose some talent.[13]

This is also interesting to notice: in bad moments, the first employees to leave the boat will be those who will find a job elsewhere more easily. So at the end of any crisis, your brightest and more valuable employees may have fled, while those who are overpaid or under-skilled will stick to their guns, as they know they won't find a similarly paid job anywhere.

> "Instead of right-sizing, our company is bright-sizing: that's when all the bright people leave"
>
> –Dilbert

Self-Direction, Self-Organization

We will discuss the concept of self-organization and how to manage it in the next chapter, but for the sake of this chapter, we will just state that self-organization, understood as having some autonomy and decision power on how to perform your job or how to organize yourself, is a key motivation factor for knowledge workers.

Self-determination theory, for instance, defines autonomy as the need to be in charge of one's own life – while still being connected and dependent on others. SDT researchers, as those quoted by Pink, conducted experiments offering external rewards for people doing tasks that intrinsically motivated them, and the result was that they lost interest in those tasks, as they became externally controlled by those offering the rewards. Hence, there was a loss of the feel of self-determination – "I am doing this in order to obtain a reward, not because I like it." Further research found that other external factors, like deadlines, which restrict and control, also decrease intrinsic motivation.

---

[13] Netflix Culture: Freedom and Responsibility (available at http://www.slideshare.net/reed2001/culture-1798664)

These researches show that when people are able to set their own deadlines and commitment and have some choice on what to work at first, as well as some decision power on the way to divide, distribute, and control their own work, they achieve better ranking in performance, quality, and motivation levels.

On the other hand, knowledge workers working on complex problems whose solution is not immediately determined and who consider themselves talented and skilled are usually de-motivated when constantly supervised or blamed when they make mistakes. As we've already discussed, command-and-control strategies are not suited for the motivation of knowledge workers or for complex problem solving; we will go deeper into the self-organization concept in the next chapter.

The Learning Enterprise

As a third motivation factor, we have the need to feel like we get better at our craft and learn new things. From a Lean perspective (Kaizen), a year without learning and improving is a lost year. From a more personal perspective, remaining at the same skill and knowledge level can create a sensation of being stuck, which can decrease motivation.

In his 2009 talk ad TED,[14] Dan H. Pink used the example of people who play musical instruments in their spare time. Why do they do that? They don't get paid! It's because they like to practice and get better at it, and that is intrinsically rewarding.

In software industries, coders are generally very vocational, with many of them having learned to code in high school or even earlier. That means that they felt the intrinsic reward of coding long before they got paid for it. Even more interesting, when I ask coders about their hobbies very frequently, they answer "coding," which means that after eight or maybe nine hours of coding at work, they will arrive home, open their laptop, and keep coding on some personal or open-source project!

But if you force them to do low-skilled tasks or repetitive projects, they will lose their motivation. This means that to use learning and competence as a motivator, you have to provide some sort of challenge suited to the skill level of your people.

---

[14] http://www.ted.com/talks/dan_pink_on_motivation.html

Sometimes the nature of your projects will be inherently boring. Several companies make a living repeating the same kind of dull software over and over, some create, read, update, and delete (CRUD) applications, and others customize the same application for different clients. In those cases, learning can still be achieved, but it has to come from sources other than the daily job. And it would be important to structure learning in these cases, because the constant repetition and low learning will slowly undermine the motivation of your workers.

Several strategies can be designed at the workplace to increase knowledge and accelerate learning even if daily tasks are repetitive. But no matter what strategy you use, either pair programming, labs, training seminars, communities of practice, Kaizen events, or self-education, my first advice would be this: structure it!

If you tell someone to read a book, he will procrastinate and never get the book read unless the learning is structured, i.e. he commits to using a defined time frame to read and sets a deadline. Some companies, for example, tell their people to invest 5% or 10% of their time on innovation and learning, but as this innovation time is not structured, people will always find more urgent things to do and complain about never having time to learn.

So, for example, if you ask your people to pair program to increase their knowledge and learn from their peers, you should ask them to set the amount of time they will invest on pair programming every week, when will they do pair programming (Wednesday morning? Every day after 3 pm?), and how will they rotate pairs according to the needs of the team and the project.

One of my favorite approaches to structured learning is to set lab time. If you commit to do 4 hours of lab time every 2 weeks, a good place to start, you'd be investing as little as 5% of your resources on innovation and learning,[15] something very difficult to be against – how much would you reduce that amount, being in a knowledge-based Agile company?

Many people ask me what are you supposed to do in lab time, so I have compiled a small list to get the ball rolling at your place and evolve from there:

---

[15] Provided you use a regular 40-h workweek.

- Design new products, proofs of concept, or prototypes.

- Implement new tools for coding, test automation, deployment, continuous integration, software quality assessment, project management, team collaboration, etc.

- Learn new programming languages or frameworks.

- Pair program and balance skills by teaching each other your personal fields of experience.

- Learn Agile programming techniques, for example, test-driven development. A good way to get started is to play ping-pong programming: we pair, I write a test, and then pass the keyboard to you, who must write the code that passes the test and refactor it. Then you write another test and pass the keyboard back to me.

- Develop a coding standard: a set of rules that everyone will follow when programming, so that the code is more readable and maintainable by everyone. A coding standard typically will include rules about code formatting, comments, naming all kinds of code elements, file management, etc.

- Read technical books and then do small seminars or presentations to explain them to your colleagues.

- Dedicate lab time to fix impediments detected in team retrospectives – technical or not.

- Work at legacy code that we never have time to refactor to make it more effective, efficient, flexible, documented, and error-free.

- Review each other's code. A good way to do it is to play the spinning bottle game: if the bottle points to you, we will collectively review your last week's code, both to spot errors or things that could be done better and to learn your best tricks.

- Develop and maintain a knowledge base system, in the form of a wiki, a blog, a lesson learned – best practices guide.

Lab time should be spent on one run, as the human brain takes some warm-up time that would make small and week-scattered ten minutes breaks of innovation highly inefficient. Again, structuring the learning time is the key: lab time should be scheduled and considered untouchable, as the temptation to use lab time to advance in the current project will be hard to resist – especially if you place lab time near the end of the iterations. That's why I usually prefer to set lab time on day one of the iteration – maybe we'd do iteration planning in the morning and then use the afternoon for lab time before actually starting the iteration.

If you want to be an Agile manager, you have to consider long term over short term every time you can. If you cancel lab time so you can meet a deadline, you'll win in the short term, but in the long term, your team will not learn and you'll create a motivational debt. On the other hand, if you don't meet the deadline (by 1 day or two, which maybe means two to four labs not canceled) most of the times, the consequences will not be that bad, while your team will be growing their competence and, in the long run, their productivity, which will make you gain back those losses in the future with interest.

This long-term approach also takes place when you promote your brightest employees and turn them into mentors for your other workers, as we saw when studying Lean management. At first, you will lose your most productive employees, but in the long run, you'll have a more productive, trained, and motivated workforce as a whole. So turning your experts into "free electrons" or "local gurus" is a good learning strategy that can also help teams coordinate and solve complex situations, as these people who were always busy are now available to help.

Another interesting approach to learning and motivation are FedEx days. Originally created at Atlassian, an Australian software company chosen as 2011's Technology Pioneer by the World Economic Forum, the goal of a FedEx day is to deliver something innovative during the next 24 h – hence the name. The format is very open: you can form a group with whoever you want and work on whatever you want as long as it is related to Atlassian products: the only rule is that you have to deliver something at the end of the 24 h. These days have provided Atlassian with a whole new set of product ideas that otherwise would never have emerged, a bunch of software fixes, and new features for existing products. Today, Atlassian is investing as much as 20% of every engineer's time in innovation and is calling for a FedEx day every quarter. This way, Atlassian fulfills the need for both self-organization and learning.

It is worth mentioning that in a company I was coaching, FedEx days were introduced, and with time, managers decided to offer a reward, in the form of a cool gadget, to the best idea or product that emerged. The results were terrible. People stopped working in things that needed to be done and designed products that they thought will give them more chances to win the gadget instead! Again, rewards are not the way to go when motivating a knowledge-based company.

Google is another company well known for asking mostly every employee to invest 20% of their time in their own projects. This is a well-known part of Google's philosophy: letting engineers spend 1 day a week working on their own side projects. They can develop new products, add new features to existing products, improve anything they like, or fix known problems.

> "Virtually everything new seems to come from the 20 percent of their time engineers here are expected to spend on side projects. They certainly don't come out of the management team."
>
> –Eric Schmidt, Google's CEO

Of course, iteration retrospectives and project postmortem analysis are a great way to learn the practical basis of what you are doing, but I feel like you can find a lot of information about them in Agile literature, so forgive me if I skip them in favor of other approaches that may complement the existing Agile body of knowledge from a more managerial perspective.

I'll end this section with an idea you must consider when designing the learning strategy for your company: mastery is an asymptote to perfection. That means that in the beginning, you learn really fast, but the better you get at something, the more difficult it is to raise your competence level. At some point, you have to decide if you want to invest more on your competence level and become a specialist or start learning something else and widen your skills. Agile structures, as we will see in the next chapters, usually prefer to broaden professional profiles than to grow hyper-specialists, but of course every case should be studied in its own circumstances.

Honor, Vision, and the Meaning of Life

Vision, purpose, honor, values, justice, and a noble cause – all of them fit into this powerful motivation area. People will be more motivated if they feel they are contributing to something greater than themselves or for the sake of only making money.

But sometimes companies have lots of trouble finding a noble cause or a strong vision that people can connect to. Then, they hire a group of consultants who will conduct a series of workshops and end up with a mission statement like:

Our mission is to continue to quickly create leading-edge metrics and continue to efficiently utilize competitive 'outside the box' thinking to allow us to authoritatively disseminate market positioning services while maintaining the highest standards.

This one was created by a random mission statement generator (available online). But surely you've got the point: most corporate visions will not trigger the intrinsic motivation of workers. They will not be motivated by things like optimizing, growing, leading, building, etc.

The power of the vision sparks when workers feel that it is consistent with their own values. That's why listing some cool values on a golden sign and placing it at the lobby will not work either. We will go deeper into this when studying corporate cultures.

Vision can happen at different levels. Maybe we can find a noble purpose for our company on a global basis: we are creating products that help people and make the world a better place. Cool! Employees will be so proud of it, and it will be a clear source of motivation. But what if the company is selling bricks? It will be very difficult to make everyone feel like we are providing homes to the people, unless the company starts some social program to provide free bricks for NGOs that are building premises for the poor. The problem in this case is that the product and the noble cause are not directly connected, and any attempt to connect them will seem artificial.

In those cases, we can search for a purpose at the market level. Maybe we are creating the coolest product, or becoming the innovation leader, or becoming a world-class company; any one of these can also motivate employees. But sometimes the company is building yet another commodity product, like toothpicks. How could someone (with all due respect) be proud of working in a toothpick factory?

Well, if you feel like that is your case, you can still find a noble vision for your people on a local or community level. Maybe your toothpick factory is contributing to the wealth of your community. Or maybe it's investing time and resources in local social projects, and that will make everyone in the company proud.

Even if your company does not contribute significantly to your local community, you can create a vision of a company where everyone will be happy to work at. You can build a corporate culture of friendship, family-work balance, fun, collaboration, comfortable workplace, a fear-free environment, etc. Your noble cause would be to create the best possible place to work at, even if you are producing toothpicks and not contributing significantly to your community. This could be reduced to a team level: your vision could be to create the best possible team in your company!

Stephen C. Lundin's book *Fish!*[16] could give you a good metaphor for this: it tells the story of a manager trying to motivate a negativity-filled workplace, who finds a fish shop at Seattle's Pike Place Market where everyone works with astonishing enthusiasm. The fishmonger teaches her about attitude, fun, and commitment at work. The moral of the story: you can make any task rewarding and find purpose in everything you do.

The noble cause, vision, or purpose is not just another marketing or communication strategy toward employees: it can create a great difference. A well-organized, committed, and efficient organization can turn into the Third Reich if the purpose is wrong!

When we study corporate culture, we will see that another important hygiene factor will be to always act according to your values, and it would be better not to engage in behaviors that go against your own sense of justice and good practice. These behaviors destroy motivation and create a sick corporate culture that will inevitably drive your company to disaster.

Connecting with Others

Finally, we have the need for social contact, acceptance, relatedness, and status. Recent studies by psychologists and neuroscientists have shown that perception of status, enhanced by praise, peer acceptance, fairness, and respect by others, can motivate people more effectively than money or formal promotions.

One important reason for it is the fact that human beings are tribal, as we've already discussed in Chap. 1 and will again discuss in the chapter on corporate culture. We feel more motivated when we get more opportunities to interact with other people, especially if they share our interests, goals, and values. Motivation indicators are much higher in people who feel that their work colleagues are like a family and declare they have friends at the workplace rather than in those who see coworkers just as that: people to cooperate with just while earning a living.

Unfortunately, software developers have grown a myth around the sociopathic *über-geek*, programming on his own at late hours, who hates social contact if it doesn't happen online. This, as you will know if you've met enough software developers, is not true. Coders enjoy social contact as

---

[16] Lundin SC (2000) Fish! A proven way to boost morale and improve results. Hyperion.

much as everyone – maybe we just tend to be passionate about our interests, and people not sharing them find us disturbing and difficult to understand, thus feeding the myth.

This myth is a killer for Agile environments. Many developers who have taught themselves how to program were individually evaluated against their classmates at college and grew up watching movies where programmers were depicted as geeky but brilliant "lone riders." Hence, they won't like to collaborate with others to create products at first. What's worse: they will be secretly afraid to seem incompetent or stupid to their colleagues.

In those cases, some companies will create special isolated environments for these "brilliant sociopaths," as they will consider them to be valuable enough to let them work outside of the teams.

Not in an Agile company.

In an Agile company, the team comes first. Period. Netflix, for example, has a policy of "No Brilliant Jerks": they see themselves as a professional sports team where everyone will assist each other all the time, and they consider that a lone star's cost to effective teamwork is too high.

Relatedness and social contact start at team level: being able to define a team identity – our team, our project – and have a status within the team. When we are able to transform a group of teams into a tribe – our tribe, our mission, our values – we maximize both networking and vision motivation factors.

In order to define team identity, several approaches can be used:

- Ask the team to choose a name for themselves, and let them develop some signs of identity, like their own customized team board and team space – or even team colors and team mascot!

- Colocate team members, which will also have the effect of better communication and team collaboration.

- Make team members engage in collaborative activities instead of individual assignments.

- Ask the team to list their values, the things they care about the most, and their mission within the company.

- Make them develop working agreements and ground rules. These protocols will be used as a common understanding of how they will behave at work and may include rules for meetings, coding style, conflict resolution, etc.

- Use meetings as ceremonies to develop the team identity. Ask them to create their own ways to handle them, which may include facilitation strategies, etiquette, or even ceremonial formulas to use.

- Encourage them to spend some time together out of the work environment. Off-site retrospectives may be a good place to start – I have coached some teams that ended up doing "barbeque retrospectives" or "swimming pool retrospectives" with outstanding results both in terms of the retrospective itself and team identity!

Apart from team networking, another great source of social contact, which can also enhance learning, is the creation of communities of practice. This means gathering all the people in the company that share a common interest or craft, for example, a community of testers: testers from all teams will have some structured time to meet and discuss testing strategies, policies, tools, etc. This will help best practices and lessons learned travel from one team to the other and also serve as a coordination and dependencies resolution space.

The Motivation of Software Developers

I would like to add some brief special advice concerning the motivation of software developers, although it may be useful for any knowledge-based environment.

Context switching and constant interruptions, I have learned, are one of the motivation hygiene factors that software environments care less about. That's the reason you see lots of developers who code while listening to music with earphones: it's their way of fighting noise and inane interruptions. But you should be aware of the research at Cornell University in the 1960s, quoted by Tom de Marco and Timothy Lister in their awesome book *Peopleware*, where they proved that coders listening to music with earphones performed more or less at the same speed as those working in a silent environment, but they were less creative and more prone to ignore global issues. That's because most programming is made on the left side of the brain, while music excites the right side and distracts it from the task performed.

Anyway, software developers need environments that help them reach flow state, or enter "the zone," as some refer to this high-concentration state. This starts with silence and respect to the people who are thinking. A way to enhance this is to ask everyone in a high-concentration state to wear some visible sign – I have used bandanas, badges, baseball caps, and, best of all, yellow safety jackets. In a team of eight, you could allow as much as six safety jackets, so anyone asking for help from the team would always be able to address at least two people, while the others remain concentrated.

The environment also should be designed to foster creativity and innovation. That means enough desk space, breakout room space, team boards to post material (mount board works fine), and as many whiteboards as you can afford – windows and office glass partitions will also serve as whiteboards if you are careful not to use permanent markers. Two screens instead of one is also a nice goodie for software developers and will get them more virtual space to work in.

Let the team members express themselves and decorate their team environment the way they like, as this will increase team identity and social motivation. Some companies care about this, as they feel the need for a good-looking, homogeneous office. To them, I would give the advice they use at American online shoe retailer Zappos: your office is not your product!

Software developers, as well as any kind of creative thinkers, need to play and freak out a bit once in a while. Forbidding or putting barriers to this kind of behavior will kill motivation as well as creativity and innovation. If you look at them severely while they are playing some ping-pong or guitar hero between concentration slots, they will probably stop doing it and go back to their computers, where you won't have a chance to know if they are doing some creative work or just updating their résumé, looking for cooler jobs online, or twitting about the boss being a jerk.

Some Motivational Anti-patterns

I will end this chapter on motivation with a list of the main anti-patterns I have found while coaching companies implementing Agile. As hygienic factors won't motivate unless they are not present (like money or enough space to work), anti-patterns won't motivate if eradicated but will kill any motivation strategy if they happen:

- *Fear.* As we've seen, fear is both a mind and a motivation killer. No motivation is possible in someone who is afraid of losing his job, being punished or yelled at, falling in disgrace, or making a fool of himself.

- *Broken promises*, my personal favorite (or anti-favorite). No matter how long you've been coaching a team, break a promise and all your previous efforts are worthless. You'll start again from the beginning but with the further difficulty of a motivational debt.

- *Irrational behavior.* Software developers and engineers in general are specially affected by irrationality, as they tend to rationally analyze every situation and usually don't know how to react to emotion-driven behaviors that go against common sense. People in panic will very often act irrationally, and this will kill motivation in people who don't understand their acts.

- *Evil.* Unfair, dishonest, greedy, selfish, or plainly illegal behavior will go against the intrinsic desire for vision, purpose, and honor.

- *Mixed signals.* If you tell people to do something and then punish them for doing it, or do the contrary yourself, you'll lose any credibility and make them feel like nothing really matters. A good example of this happens when a company writes its values and mission statement but then acts in a way that is not consistent with them, or tells people that they are "empowered" but then doesn't let them take any risks or decisions – be careful and walk your talk!

- *Treat them as resources.* A usual trap to fall into this anti-pattern is to define "resource pools" and draw people from the pool as you need them or arbitrarily reassign them from one project to another, making them feel like inter-exchangeable parts of a mechanism. People need to feel like they are making a noticeable contribution, and using them as commodities will not fulfill that need.

- *Giving hell and bullying.* Nobody has ever felt motivated after someone yelled at him for a good while. What is worse: yelling at someone who can't fight back because you are the boss is a form of bullying, as well as a lack of respect and a use of fear as a supposed management tool.

- *Micromanagement, command-and-control.* As we showed in the beginning of this chapter, Taylor-style structures of telling everyone what to do, how exactly to do it, and then supervising and controlling everyone will, again, make people feel like parts of a mechanism and not as creative thinkers contributing to a common enterprise.

- *Overcommitment*. Setting impossible deadlines will make the team think that they are not performing adequately and that their point of view, their estimations, and their concerns are not taken seriously by their managers.

- *Divide and conquer*. Setting your people one against the other so they fight themselves and don't join forces against you will maybe qualify you to rule a tiny Italian kingdom during the Renaissance, or a small fief in Japan's Sengoku period, but not to manage an Agile team and make your company grow and improve.

- *Zero-sum bonuses and incentives*. When there's a fixed pot of money to divide between people depending on their performance, they will feel like the money others are earning is the money that they won't, so everyone will be so concerned about their own reward that collaboration and teamwork will be seriously damaged.

- *Zealotry and arrogance*. When only one opinion counts – the manager's – and no questioning is allowed, there's no chance that people will engage, be committed, and feel empowered. A collaborative environment calls for everyone's opinion and contribution. As a manager, sometimes you'll have to let them go their way even if you feel like there's a better one and try to be humble and admit that, no matter how sure you feel about something, sometimes you just won't be right.

- *Office politics*. Criticizing coworkers, scheming, stealing ideas, deceiving, backstabbing, influencing, and manipulating others in order to gain power and status – these activities will consume time and resources and won't create any value. Furthermore, they will create a sick environment to work in and kill collaboration.

- *Gossip*. This can be a social activity, but most of the time, it is harmful, as it will break people's intimacy, create rumors, introduce erroneous information, make other people suspicious about what you are mumbling about, create a negative environment, distract you from work, make you feel distressed because of the uncertainty of the information, and, ultimately, kill trust between coworkers. Gossiping has also been identified as a great source of stress.

- *Information control*. Organizations are said to be as mature as information is free to flow through them. When information is not available, you are telling people that they are not mature, skilled, or important enough to access it, and hence, their perception of status, autonomy, and competence will be damaged.

- *Priority changes*. Most human beings need some stability in their environment. If urgent requests, emergencies, and priority changes are constantly arriving, people will have a constant feeling of uncertainty and "what's coming next?". This can be right for a firemen squad or a hospital, but when you are part of a software development team, this is not what you should expect.

Summary

Happy companies have lower turnover rates, lower absenteeism, lower stress indexes, better outside references, better customer loyalty, and higher quality of life. Even longer employee's life expectancy, as a definite correlation between happiness and health, has been established by scientists.[17]

As you have seen, motivating your organization is not just a matter of setting a bonus policy, printing some inspirational posters with cool slogans, and, once a year, firing up an employee party. It's more of a full-time job.

Team leaders and Agile coaches can help managers on a daily basis in the goal to maintain a high level of motivation and morale, but the overall motivation strategy for the organization should be set by management. The good news is that the science of motivation has advanced vastly in the last decades, so now you have a body of knowledge you can rely on to design your motivation strategy.

As shown, the impact of motivation on company results, culture, and performance is so high that many Agile companies are turning their "happiness index" into their main performance indicator, constantly tuning their processes and policies to maximize it. In fact, some companies have turned their old-style human resources departments into employee happiness departments, even appointing chief happiness officers!

Things to Try

- Several practices have been described in this chapter. Make a list of them, make sure to review them thoroughly, and discuss them with your team.

- List the five motivational areas (security, self-organization, learning, vision, networking) and ask your people to rank their degree of

---

[17] Kageyama J (2009) Happiness and sex difference in life expectancy. Max Planck Institute for Demographic Research Working Paper WP-2009-009.

satisfaction in each one from 1 to 10. For every mark under ten, they should write a short paragraph starting with "to make it a ten, I would." Use it to design your motivation strategy for that person.

• Set a happiness index. Ask everyone to rate from one to ten how happy they feel. Trace your happiness index on a chart during the year and notice how different events affect general happiness.

• Find a way to get rid of financial rewards, bonuses, and variable salaries. Period.

• Strive to create interruption-free environments. Ask your people to define protocols to deal with interruptions and post them where everyone can see them. Then ask them to follow up on them, reporting when the protocol has been violated, and seeing what could be enhanced to deal with such violations.

• Research on Agile office space. Several Agile offices have been described and reported online, with lots of ideas on how to create collaboration spaces. Give some budget and some autonomy to your people so they can customize their own Agile space.

• Structure your learning. Start by setting a fixed and scheduled time for lab. Ask your people to design a lab strategy and think how they are going to show the results and defend the return of investment on learning.

• Ask your people to brainstorm a list of not less than 50 values (honesty, learning, customer focus, integrity, teamwork, positive attitude, politeness, collaboration, courage, etc. You can even search online for lists of team values). Then make them vote the ones that they care for the most – ideally not less than four but no more than nine. For each value, ask them to write short stories and examples of what they do and don't to honor those values – especially if they can point to real cases. Post your team values where everyone can see them and use them on retrospectives and other team ceremonies to keep an eye on what's important.

• As recommended in the chapter on Agile and Lean, start a Kaizen program scheduling regular Kaizen events, in the form of team retrospectives, project postmortem analysis, general workouts, etc. You can find a lot of information on Kaizen events and their formats online or on Agile/Lean literature.

• Design your team's skills matrix (search online for the topic). This is a matrix with your people on a vertical axis and a list of the skills needed to perform your projects on a horizontal axis. Everyone in the team will fill their row marking, on every cell representing a given skill, if they find themselves proficient, so-so, or have no idea on that area. Try to find skills that are known to only one person: that will mean that if that person is missing, your team will be compromised. Design pairing strategies so this person teaches other team members that specific skill, making your team more robust and enhancing competence.

- For every person you are managing, codesign a learning program in the long term. The Agile coach can help you with this task, as he will be following it on a daily basis.

- Discuss with your people if they would like to engage in some community or social program. If they feel like that would give them a higher sense of purpose, try to make some company resources available. Maybe you can lend training rooms, host a website for a NGO, volunteer some time, sponsor a social initiative, organize quarterly information events, etc.

- Join or launch an open-source initiative. It will give your people an opportunity to try new things without much risk and can also be a great and affordable marketing for your company.

- Print the anti-pattern list and ask everyone you manage to anonymously rank your de-motivational index, with 0 being "you never do that" and 10 being "yeah, that's you all the time." Use it to start a self-improvement program as an Agile manager. And don't kill the messengers!

- Launch a 360° evaluation – you can find a lot of resources about them online. Ask your bosses, your coworkers, and the people you are managing to evaluate your management style. Don't argue back: accept whatever they tell you as the truth, and commit to work on your improvement areas.

- Define your company's noble cause. Don't do it only by yourself – ask everyone to participate, submitting their views on how they feel they are doing something that matters.

- Try to encourage team identity and team diversity while tightly aligning every team on a common goal.

- Launch inter-team communities of practice. Let everyone join the community they like, despite their current skills or job title.

- Encourage your people to network with other colleagues through conferences, online forums and mailing lists, local groups, etc.

Recommended Readings

Csikszentmihalyi M (1991) Flow: the psychology of optimal experience. Harper Perennial, New York

Jericó P (2009) No fear: in business and in life. Palgrave Macmillan, New York

Lundin SC (2000) Fish! A Proven Way to Boost Morale and Improve Results. Hyperion, New York

Maslow AH (1970) Motivation and personality. Joanna Cotler Books, New York

McGregor D (1960) The human side of the enterprise. McGraw Hill, New York

Pink DH (2009) Drive: the surprising truth about what motivates us. Riverhead Hardcover, New York

Reiss S (2002) Who am I? The 16 basic desires that motivate our actions and define our personalities. Berkley Trade, New York

Wenger E (1999) Communities of practice: learning, meaning, and identity. Cambridge University Press, London

Wenger E (2002) Cultivating communities of practice. Harvard Business Review Press, Boston

Self-Organization

From Roman Legions to Guerrillas

5

Letting the Team Go

As we've already seen, command-and-control and hierarchical military-style management has been the prevalent paradigm for centuries. It survived during the industrial revolution, but as it happened with classical military operations that evolved from the brutal clash of well-formed battalions to guerrilla-style warfare, command-and-control management started to tumble down when the information society was born and the rise of knowledge workers changed the world's economy.

3M's CEO and visionary William L. McKnight questioned his colleagues on why they hired talented people and then spent all the time telling them how they should be doing their stuff. He was one of a group of visionaries who, in the early 1950s, envisioned a new way of managing companies based on innovation, initiative, and collaboration.

> "As our business grows, it becomes increasingly necessary to delegate responsibility and to encourage men and women to exercise their initiative. This requires considerable tolerance. Those men and women, to whom we delegate authority and responsibility, if they are good people, are going to want to do their jobs in their own way.
>
> Mistakes will be made. But if a person is essentially right, the mistakes he or she makes are not as serious in the long run as the mistakes management will make if it undertakes to tell those in authority exactly how they must do their jobs.
>
> *(continued)*

Á. Medinilla, *Agile Management*, DOI 10.1007/978-3-642-28909-5_5,
© Springer-Verlag Berlin Heidelberg 2012

> Management that is destructively critical when mistakes are made kills initiative. And it's essential that we have many people with initiative if we are to continue to grow."
>
> –William W. McKnight (circa 1948)

Self-organization is a precondition for successful Agile or Lean initiatives. As we've also seen, self-organization is an important motivation factor, so the question is not if we should let the team self-organize, but how to do it and still make them work in a way that makes the organization successful.

According to my own experience, when attempting self-organization two main problems arise from a management perspective: lack of trust in the team to perform adequately and fear that they won't do what the manager considers to be the best thing to do. In the background, the manager will also worry that his role and status will be diminished if he is not allowed to command his people, and he will also be afraid that he will not know what to do with all the time that he currently spends controlling his people. This set of difficulties is usually referred to as "the problem of letting go."

Considering all the woes that come from management when it comes to self-organization, one would be tempted to ask: Isn't there a way to be Agile without self-organization? If we have a smart manager who is into the Agile thing, why don't we let him command a team and tell them how to do Agile stuff?

Delegation Is Not a Zero-Sum Game

First thing we have to make sure is that all managers understand that power delegation is not subtracting any power from themselves, as power is not a finite resource. In fact, the more you delegate, the more power you create. If you manage people who have the power to make decisions, you are managing a group of more empowered or powerful people, so your own power and status grow bigger.

Another way of looking at this fact is that no matter how much you delegate, you are still accountable and responsible for the tasks you are delegating. Delegating some responsibility does not make you less responsible: the task is commissioned to you, you are the one delegating it, it is your decision, and if the person you delegate it to fails, you'll still be accountable for the failure.

Effective delegation is, in fact, one of the crucial challenges of successful managers. The problem with delegation is a vicious circle: if you don't delegate tasks because you are afraid that your employees won't perform them adequately (sometimes meaning that maybe they'll do them in a different way than the one you prefer), you do them yourself. That means you are always busy, so you don't have time to train your people and show them how to do these kinds of tasks. On the other hand, they don't get a chance to practice because you are so afraid that they will fail, like anyone who is learning how to do something for the first time. So they remain ignorant in your eyes, and next time a task arrives, again you won't delegate, thus closing the circle.

As you see, to make your people grow, you have to delegate and give trust slightly in advance, meaning that you trust them to do a good job a bit before they can actually perform adequately. You have to always delegate tasks to your team one step beyond their own capability, but not further!

Complex Environments

In Chap. 2, when studying Agile genealogy, we established that most modern knowledge-based companies are operating in complex environments. The difference between simple and complex is not the same as the difference between easy and difficult: building an airplane is difficult, but it falls into the domain of simple problems because the problem is known and the solution is known too. Airplane builders have a detailed blueprint where every single piece is thoroughly described, including mounting instructions. Even more, this month they are probably building the same kind of airplane they built a month ago. Workers perform a defined set of tasks over and over, so the outcome of every task is very predictable.

On the other hand, software developers very seldom have this kind of situation. The problem and its solution are presented in the form of a set of fuzzy requirements that tend to change and grow during the project, a phenomenon known as "scope creep." And no project I have ever known started with a perfect definition of every single class, method, routine, and variable – because that would be the source code, and then the only duty of the developer would be to type it.

In this kind of environment, predicting the results is like trying to see into the future. That is why all estimations on software projects are sort of "guesstimates": we don't have complete information, we start with some guess that we know is uncertain, and we should be adapting as we learn more about the project. The whole Agile approach is based on this.

Complexity science teaches us that the adaptive approach is preferred over the predictive approach in a complex system. Trying to use predictive approaches in complex systems is like trying to program a car to go from home to the office at rush hour with no reaction capability: it will very surely crash into another car or bump into a pedestrian crossing the street. To manage traffic, we should be able to tell the car where we want to go and then let it figure out when to stop and when to accelerate depending on non-predictable events like cars, traffic lights, and pedestrians.

Which leads to my loved topic of roundabouts and self-organization.

The Problem with Central Intelligence

One of the most used examples of a self-organizing system in Agile literature is the roundabout. A roundabout is a system with a very reduced set of rules:

1. Don't crash (this is usually a good rule).
2. Follow the roundabout circulation direction.
3. Cars in the roundabout have preference.
4. Exit the roundabout only from the outer lane.[1]

General traffic rules also apply, but in essence, roundabouts leave all the decisions on when to enter or exit to the drivers. And they work. Very effectively, in fact. In many situations, they have proven to be safer, provide better traffic flow, and have a higher capacity than other solutions like traffic lights, where cars must wait until the light turns green even if there are no other cars crossing.

Of course, when an accident occurs or an obstacle blocks the roundabout, traffic agents are required to deal with the impediment. But what happens when the traffic police agents decide to manage the road intersections?

---

[1] Drivers in Spain seem to have some trouble with this last rule and often rally across the whole roundabout using all available space. Be careful when driving in roundabouts there!

Well, first we have to consider the cost of having a policeman managing all traffic junctions. The management overhead can be prohibitive. But even if we wanted to make such an investment, there is another problem we have to consider too: if the traffic is low, the policeman can make good decisions on who has the right to enter the junction, but when the traffic gets higher, each individual driver is capable of assessing his own chances to pass or enter the junction, while the policeman is not able to process that much information. So he usually allows a big batch of cars to pass, until the other cars start to honk aggressively, and then he will switch to those. As the batches grow bigger, the traffic jam will become inevitable!

As you see, the problem with central intelligence is that, no matter how well trained and skilled it is, it can't contain and process all the information in the system. In fact, no one can.

If you look into nature, you'll find it hard to locate examples of central intelligence, meaning that one smart element will tell every other part of the system what to do. On the contrary, a lot of decentralized intelligence or "swarm intelligence" examples exist, from ant colonies to bird flocking, fish schooling, bacterial growth, or immune systems. In fact, swarm intelligence has been replicated on robotics as the best way to manage decentralized self-organizing systems.

Swarm intelligence, as most complex adaptive systems, relies on a small set of rules that allow individuals a great deal of autonomy as long as they follow those rules. For instance, bird flocking seems to work with three simple rules:

1. Separation – avoid crowding neighbors (short-range repulsion).
2. Alignment – steer toward average heading of neighbors.
3. Cohesion – steer toward average position of neighbors (long-range attraction).[2]

In other example, ants looking for food will follow a set of simple rules that can be summarized as:

1. While walking randomly out of the hive, leave a pheromone trail.
2. If you find a pheromone trail, follow it and lay more pheromone.
3. If you reach home while following a pheromone trail, turn back.
4. If you find food, turn back and follow the pheromone trail back home.
   This set can be reduced to as much as two rules:

---

[2] Tanner HG, Jadbabaie A, Pappas GJ (2003) Stable flocking of mobile agents, Part I: Fixed topology. 42nd IEEE Conference on Decision and Control 2:2010–2015.

1. If not carrying food, walk randomly or on a pheromone trail in food direction.
2. If carrying food, walk on pheromone trail in home direction.[3]

> "Simple, clear purpose and principles give rise to complex and intelligent behavior. Complex rules and regulations give rise to simple and stupid behavior."
>
> –Dee Hock, CEO Emeritus VISA International

So the question is this: central intelligence is great when we face predictive, simple, algorithmic environments. But when we live in a complex, unpredictable environment, self-organization works better. So much better that one of the most well-known examples of central intelligence, the CIA, is looking at complex adaptive systems theory (one of the sources of Agile lore) to find ways to operate in a security environment that, by its nature, is changing rapidly in ways they cannot predict.[4]

Self-Organization Is Not Self-Management

As we said in Chap. 3, a self-organizing team is not the same as a self-managed team, and self-management is not a necessary condition for Agile. In fact, as far as I know, self-management is still to be proved in big enterprise environments.

To express the difference between self-organization and self-management, and also in order to better understand how to manage self-organizing teams, we can use the example of the roundabout again. As you remember, the roundabout had a very small set of rules. And if some accident happens, traffic agents will be called in to cope with the situation.

Well... There you are! Rule setting and impediment removal are two of the things that a self-organizing team is probably not able to do on its own.

---

[3] Goss S, Aron S, Deneubourg JL, Pasteels JM (1989) Self-organized shortcuts in the argentine ant. Naturwissenschaften 76:579–581.

[4] Calvin AD (2007) Toward a complex adaptive intelligence community. C.I.A. Center for the Study of Intelligence.

The underlying idea on self-organization is that a behavior will emerge from the system without a central intelligence planning and imposing it. But notice that we are talking about not imposing a *behavior*, not goals, boundaries, constraints, or primal rules. These boundaries, constraints, and rules might be imposed by the environment, in the case of a self-managed team: they have a given pool of resources (budget, skills, tools), and they have to conform to market and legal rules.

In the case of medium to big organizations, management might be needed to align the behaviors of self-organized teams to implement the organization's strategy and meet its goals. But imposing the desired behavior will kill self-organization, reducing motivation and making an Agile emergent pattern impossible.

> "We had management in engineering. And the structure was tending to tell people, 'No, you can't do that.' So Google got rid of the managers. Now most engineers work in teams of three, with project leadership rotating among team members. If something isn't right, even if it's in a product that has already gone public, teams fix it without asking anyone.
>
> For a while, I had 160 direct reports. No managers. It worked because the teams knew what they had to do. That set a cultural bit in people's heads: You are the boss. Don't wait to take the hill. Don't wait to be managed.
>
> And if you fail, fine. On to the next idea. There's faith here in the ability of smart, well-motivated people to do the right thing. Anything that gets in the way of that is evil."
>
> –Wayne Rosing, Google VP of Engineering 2001–2005

The Self-Organizing Team

So if we want to manage knowledge-based teams performing in complex non-predictable environments, we need them to self-organize in order to obtain better results. Self-organization, from this perspective, means that a small set of rules will be set, maybe by management alone or maybe by collaboration between management and the team depending on its maturity. A set of boundaries of constraints defined by the company, the market, the product, the client, and other team-external factors will also be in place, and then a company-strategy aligned goal will be set for the team, and we will expect them to find the best way to achieve that goal without imposing external criteria, planning, or authority.

Some degree of commitment is needed from the team to make self-organization happen. Many managers fear that if they don't interfere frequently with the team's dynamic, they will just lag around until it's too late to steer the project to a safe harbor. If this is really the case, probably a previous investment in motivation and education is needed so the team understands the advantages of working in a more Agile way.

During this period of Agile adaption and team maturing, progressive delegation should take place. This means that self-organization is not a binary condition: on the contrary, several degrees of self-organization can be achieved. Maybe you start by asking them how they would do something and make their opinion count while you still remain as the one taking the decision. Then you could start to participate in team decisions as one more opinion, and later you could tell them to decide and inform you of their decisions and their reasoning for taking it.

On another dimension, different tasks or management areas can be at different delegation levels. Maybe you let them fully decide on task estimations, participate with them in the improvement plan design, ask them about project priorities before you decide, and, still, be the only one deciding on salaries and budget allocation.

Not understanding these two progressive dimensions of delegation creates a lot of trouble when managing self-organizing teams. I have met several managers who asked their teams to implement an Agile framework and self-organize, only to see their team say, "as a self-organizing team, we've decided we hate Agile and we've gone back to waterfall." In this case, the team is showing a low-maturity behavior, so the delegation level was clearly excessive. Probably these managers should start by deciding on their own that an Agile framework is to be implemented and then asking the team about the best way to do it, what framework to choose, or the best way to train everyone. "Agile framework," in this case, would be a context set by management, and it is within that context that we expect the team to self-organize.

Managing Self-Organizing Teams

This last example helps me introduce the way of managing self-organized teams, which is to set a good context and let them figure out the rest.

Setting a good context is the key for self-organization to be successful. Many managers tell their teams "go self-organize!" and slam their office door, while forgetting to set a good context, and they are later on surprised to see that their teams did something really stupid.

> "Managers: when one of your talented people does something dumb, don't blame them. Instead, ask yourself what context you failed to set."
>
> –Netflix Culture

A few years ago, I was coaching a manager who was absolutely upset because he had installed an electric grill in the office kitchen so employees could toast their sandwiches or maybe even cook something simple, and just one day later someone decided to grill sardines, creating a huge and dirty mess in the kitchen and making the whole office stink of fish.

The response of the manager was to remove the grill and shut down the whole kitchen thing. But of course, this was not an intelligent move, as everyone else in the office was upset because Sardine-Boy's mistake had cost them the use of the kitchen, and they also saw the manager's decision as tyrannical. In a second lecture, what the manager was unconsciously telling the employees was, "we don't tolerate failure here – not even once," creating a fear-filled environment where everyone was afraid of trying new things because they could fail, be punished, and look stupid to other colleagues.

This situation could have been avoided by setting a good context:

1. The electric grill is here to provide you better meals at work. Feel free to use it in any way you imagine!
2. You must leave the electric grill in the same state you found it and ready to be used by anyone who comes after you.
3. Kitchen activities should not affect the rest of the office in any way.

As you see, a good context includes a small and simple set of rules that allows a lot of freedom to the team, as well as a small set of boundaries and constraints that prevent unwanted behavior.

Bad context for self-organization would be, for example, "You must not cook anything but sandwiches in the electric grill." This is imposing some-one else's policy and not allowing the team any kind of self-organizing space (other than the content of the sandwich). Control mechanisms, top-down decision making, or asking for management approval should be avoided for a self-organization culture to emerge.

When setting a higher-level context related to the team's job, you must take into account several aspects:

- Alignment with corporate policy and strategy, as well as with your vision and values
- Clear goal definition: success criteria and metrics
- Key stakeholders and their role
- Level of priority and required quality
- Main boundaries and constraints
- Rules that apply

Goal setting is a particularly relevant art when defining context. Agile literature has often referred to the SMART (Specific, Measurable, Achievable, Realistic, Time-boxed) and INVEST (Independent, Negotiable, Valuable, Estimable, Small, Testable) acronyms for good goal setting.

Good goals affect team behavior positively. Proposers of goal setting theory (Latham and Locke 2002; Shalley 1995)[5,6] have found several ways in which goals influence performance, including focusing attention on priority issues, inducing higher effort when goals are ambitious yet achievable, maintaining the work pace to meet goals, or enhancing creative thinking and motivation, as pursuing a goal will be more rewarding than just following commands.

Intra-entrepreneurs and ROWE

In some ways, what we are trying is to turn a team of individually commanded people into "Team Inc.," a micro-company within the company. When you deal with suppliers, you tell them what you need, when you need it, and the success and quality criteria that are associated with your request, thus creating a valid context, maybe through a project contract. Sometimes you put some control mechanisms in place if you don't trust the

---

[5] Latham GP, Locke EA (2002) Building a practically useful theory of goal setting and task motivation. Am Psychol 57:705–717.

[6] Shalley CE (1995) Effects of coaction, expected evaluation, and goal setting on creativity and productivity. Acad Manag J 38(2):483–503.

supplier very much, or maybe setting some way of frequently looking at how things are going is enough, but you surely won't be personally addressing all your supplier's employees who are related to the project telling them what to do and how you want them to do it – unless you are managing your suppliers in a Taylor-Ford way!

Some companies are even experimenting with the concept of intra-entrepreneurship. They are finding out that some of their more talented and brighter employees have left the company, even if they were happy with their job, because they had a higher need of autonomy and challenge, so they decided to quit and start their own business, very often in the same field they were working in. So these companies have decided to provide these *entrepreneur wannabes* with the environment they need, but inside the company: sometimes in the form of a spin-off company, sometimes as an autonomous internal program or a separate business unit. These intra-entrepreneurs are given some resources, full autonomy on how best to use them, and some goals with a success criteria.

In other cases, companies are realizing that controlling their employees through time sheets and access cards to make sure that everyone is at his desk for 8 hours a day is becoming obsolete and useless in a world of road warriors, telecommuters and ubiquitous broadband. In fact offices made more sense when people didn't have computers, printers, fax machines, mobile phones, and Internet access at home.

The average telecommuter is more productive, gets more flow time during the day, has a better family-work balance, and less chances to quit and go to another company that doesn't allow telecommuting. Telecommuting boosts motivation through autonomy, saves costs for the company, and is better for the environment (less transport means less pollution). On the other hand, most offices have been proven to kill employee's flow because of constant interruptions, noise, useless meetings, etc. The benefits of telecommuting are overwhelming and vastly covered by research.

So what some companies are doing is to promote Results-Only Work Environments or ROWE, a human resource strategy originally created by Jody Thompson and Cali Ressler at Best Buy,[7] where employees are not paid by the number of hours worked but for tangible results.

---

[7] http://www.gorowe.com/. At my current company, Proyectalis, we practice a 100% ROWE, with associates getting paid for the projects they deliver. There's no hour count or holiday policy, and we even got rid of physical offices, as we have people working scattered all around the globe.

Other companies are transforming their offices from a cubicle-farm-like environment to a more collaborative space where telecommuters can meet periodically when they need closer interaction and collaboration. In fact, it is becoming more and more common to have offices with less space than employees, as most of them are supposed to be working at home, and freelancing is considered by many experts to be the next big trend in knowledge-based job markets.

So, as you see, learning to manage self-organizing teams is not only a matter of enabling Agility, but also to cope with twenty-first-century workplaces!

Radical Self-Organization

How far should self-organization go? Well, results show that as long as you go gradually, the sky is the limit!

For instance, consider Netflix. They reached a point where hours worked per day or week were not being tracked, as they realized that everyone was working online overnight, on weekends, or even during vacations. But then someone pointed out that, while they were not tracking hours worked, they still tracked vacation days per year.

Traditional managers would have answered "Of course! If we didn't do that, people would take more vacations than they are allowed to." But, as pointed out, people were also working during vacations, so should they deduct those hours from holiday time and add it later on? Maybe they should not be allowed to work on holidays?

Netflix managers solution was aligned with their policy of freedom, responsibility, and self-organization: they declared that there was no vacation policy. Period.

When they explain that, other people not in their company stare at them and sometimes ask "Aren't you afraid that people will misbehave if there is not a vacation policy?" Their answer: "There is also no clothing policy at Netflix, but no one comes to work naked. Lesson: you don't need policies for everything." Later on, they also introduced a policy for expenses, entertainment, gifts, and travel that reads: *"Act in Netflix's Best Interest"* – five words long!

Let's see another example of radical self-organization. At Semco, a Brazilian company with over 200 million dollars in revenue and with a double-digit growth during the last 10 years, a sort of industrial democracy has been instituted. There are no secretaries or assistants – everyone will take care of his personal stuff. There is no human resource department, and teams will hire their managers and not the other way around. Any employee is free to attend management board meetings and participate with his own ideas, and all economic information, including salaries or profits, is publicly available.

One of the most controversial decisions at Semco is to let everyone set their own salary. Ricardo Semler, owner and alma mater of the revolutionary Semco management style, often says that when they decided to go that way, everyone told him he was insane. They assumed that people would always try to set the highest possible salary, as human nature is to be greedy and selfish. But that has not been Semco's experience at all. Very rarely did someone set a salary for himself that was above the expected, and sometimes people even set a salary for themselves that was under the company's first expectation.

"Treat them as responsible and well informed adults" is Semler's motto. For him, five things are needed to set a fair salary: there are three known by the company and two by the employee. The first three are the average market salary for someone performing that particular job, how much other colleagues at the company earn for that job, and how much the company can afford to pay right now according to their budget and resources. The two that the employee knows are how much they would like to earn at this moment of their career and how much the people of their personal environment with similar background and experience are earning. So giving the first three to the employees, they have all the information available to make a good decision.[8]

To understand the salary dynamic at Semco, you have to understand that everyone knows what everyone else is paid, so there is a peer pressure factor, and as everyone also has access to the company numbers, they know that salaries account for most of their operating costs. So if they set too high a salary, most colleagues will see them as a way of solving a budget problem. Another way of viewing this under the self-organization perspective is that employees are given all the information on resources, environment, goals, and such, so an effective context is being set to take the correct decision.

---

[8] Semler R (1995) Maverick: the success story behind the world's most unusual workplace. Grand Central Publishing.

Employees at Semco receive as much as 23% share of their own business unit's quarterly profit. How they divide that money between the business unit members is up to them – they can either make equal parts or decide who deserves more. They can even decide to keep the money for other purposes like loans to workers or education. These decisions will be made every quarter, so if they mess something up, the amount won't be so big, and they will have several opportunities to correct it. All this is being done without management involvement.

But Semco's radical environment didn't emerge overnight: it is the result of more than 20 years of gradual delegation of power and corporate culture building. So the lessons on the Semco experiment to self-organization could be:

1. Treat employees as responsible and well-informed adults.
2. Provide enough context.
3. Delegate progressively over time.

Visibility and Reporting in an Agile Environment

Trusting the team to self-organize is not the same as leaving them alone for months and not caring about the progress of the project or the impediments they are facing. You'll need to manage some kind of information to help the team make the most out of their abilities. But, on the other hand, mostly everyone on earth hates to report. This is especially true when it comes to knowledge workers on Agile teams, and even more if the report is asked through a heavyweight, bureaucratic, and time-consuming process.

On self-organizing Agile teams, report requests can be seen as an attempt to control and supervise the team, so you are in danger of killing self-organization. Furthermore, reports kill motivation as they reduce the perceived autonomy of individuals.

You must remember that reports are waste: they don't add value to the product or service you are delivering. Your client will seldom perceive the difference in the number or quality of reports issued while creating two similar products. Many times I have faced the prevalent paradigm that reports were needed for normal operations, only to see how normal operations went on – or even improved – when reports were removed. On these occasions, every time a paradigm is shifted, there were many people in cognitive dissonance trying to forge arguments in favor of reports: "If we don't have them, the sky will fall on our heads." The truth, many times, is that they've seen reports everywhere for decades, and now they can't imagine a report-free work environment. Or they even fear that having no reports will make them look nonprofessional to clients.

I must admit anyway that, while they are Lean waste, sometimes the information reports provide is useful for optimal decision making – although I'm sure there are different ways an Agile manager could gather that information himself without bothering or interfering with the team. So the question is, as with all forms of waste, which is the minimum set of reports we need, if we need reports at all.

To reduce the amount of control, increase the perceived autonomy and self-organization of the team, and improve the effectiveness of the value stream, Agile companies are successfully using all sorts of visual management tools to replace traditional reports. In the usual Kanban or Scrum board, for example, the current state of an iteration of work is showed with plenty of detail: pending tasks, tasks they are working at, tasks completed, remaining work until the end of the iteration, etc. As the Agile coach helps the team mature, they usually incorporate more information into the board. I have helped to engineer boards including information such as:

- Name of the team and list of team members, coach, and project manager/ product owner.

- Description of the project they are working at.

- List of the work packages/product backlog for the project they are working at, with estimations, iteration allocation, and predicted delivery dates (release plan).

- Amount of work committed for this iteration and its progress – sometimes through the use of burn-down charts.

- Unplanned items that the team encountered or were commissioned to handle during the iteration – sometimes with a list of the people who are interrupting the team the most and the percentage of time they are investing on those unplanned items.

- Who is working on each task.

- How many tasks one person is handling – context switching or multitasking indicators.

- Date and hour when each task entered the different states of the value stream – usually handwritten on the Kanban card. This helps to obtain average lead time, cycle time, idle time, and other valuable information that can also be shown in the board, and even create historical data in the form of histograms that, again, can be available at the board.

- Historical and current team's capacity, sometimes in the form of velocity (man/hours, story points or average features per iteration).

- Task nature and priority.

- Blocked tasks and nature of the impediment.

- Tasks in queues (waiting for some event or free resource).

- Definition of "Done" – when can they claim that something is fully done (documented, tested, validated...).

- Paper prototypes, wireframes, and other low-fidelity sketches of the product.

- Main impediments and what they are doing to cope with them.

- Description of their way of working, ground rules, or working agreements.

- Scheduled meetings, both regular (daily stand-up, iteration planning, iteration review, team retrospective) and specifically scheduled meetings.

- Motivation of the team members during iteration (some ways of doing this are the emotional seismograph or the Niko-niko calendar).

Seems like plenty of information to me! And one of the many great things about Agile boards is that instead of asking a project manager for a report every 2 weeks that will take him some hours to write, the board gets updated every 24 h in a simple 10-minute collaborative stand-up meeting that the team values and appreciates. By the way, attending those meetings is a good and inexpensive way of keeping up with the team and providing guidance and help if needed.

Another approach, as we saw in Chap. 2, are A3 reports. Usually associated with a problem-solving technique that originated at Toyota, A3 reports are in fact a wider concept of reducing report waste by using one A3-sized paper (twice the size of the regular sheet of paper, or A4) to standardize a series of work forms – the problem-solving process just used an A3 as many other processes and reports at Toyota.

The A3-thinking pattern encouraged by Toyota made everyone focus on the important facts to report instead of introducing unnecessary literature and art on them. The usual A3 report was laser beam targeted on the situation, goal, observed facts, ideas for improvement, and implementation plan – and it must fit into an A3, so this is a way of looking for "as less reports as possible."

One way to start an A3 report in your Agile team could be to ask them to replicate the most relevant and midterm information on their board on an A3. But never underestimate the impact of wandering through the different team spaces looking at their boards and coming up with some questions on how to help them – that's true Genchi Genbutsu or Gemba Walk!

If you go-and-see, one of the usual translations for Genchi Genbutsu, very possibly you'll bump into facts that very seldom make their way to an official report, as few people write a report about the broken air conditioner or the server that is painfully slow. On the other hand, I have seen great Agile teams de-motivated because nobody took the time to look at their thoroughly engineered team board, maybe just to tell them "hey, good job!" In a particularly sad but proactive and brilliant case, the team posted a sign on the board that read, "If you are a manager and you are reading this, please tell us: we would like to buy you a coffee."

Please, be that manager. Office coffee is not that bad when it brings peace, comfort, and some managerial support to your teams.

Summary

Self-organization is possibly one of the toughest parts of Agile management. Everyone loves to motivate, design teams and structures, or even run retrospectives and Kaizen events, but when it comes to letting the team go and take some risks, we usually think twice.

The let-go of the team must happen gradually. If you give them too much freedom in advance, they will very probably mess things up. You have to understand that most of the people have never ever taken that kind of responsibility: they went to the school, high school and college their parents decided on. Many times they even studied for a career suggested by them. They joined the first company that hired them, and they probably followed orders blindly for some years. And now we are going Agile and asking them to self-organize, take decisions, and run into risks. It is no surprise that some of them go into shock and denial for months!

Every step you take to make the team more self-organized must be planned and well defined. Before you ask them to self-organize, you have to make sure that the adequate context has been set through simple rules, goals, boundaries, and constraints, and that the context has been thoroughly discussed with the team.

Self-organization, we have seen, is not a binary yes-no condition. Telling them to self-organize does not dismiss you from your duties as a manager, and giving them some authority won't lessen your accountability. To keep yourself informed and close to the team, boards, A3 reports, and informal meetings can be used instead of heavyweight bureaucratic processes.

One last thing: be sure you are prepared, for if you unleash the force of the self-organizing Agile team, the sky is the limit for the things you can achieve!

Things to Try

- Think of the self-organization model that your Agile implementation is using right now. Are they self-organizing enough? No matter how self-organized they are right now, remember you should always help them move one step further. Ask them to create a board with the rules, boundaries, and constraints that they must follow, and then all the things they can decide and self-organize about. Review it with them and discuss how they can increase their autonomy.

- A good way to do this is to find online Jurgen Appelo's "Delegation Poker" game and play it with your people or other managers. Discuss with them your current delegation levels and seek ways to move it one step further. Learn also about his delegation board concept and try to implement it at your company.

- If your company is looking for new markets, products, or ways of making money, start an intra-entrepreneur program. Intra-entrepreneurs should behave as real entrepreneurs, finding a suitable idea, creating the "elevator pitch" for the idea, designing a business model, and finding sponsorship inside the company to create and manage a business unit.

- Design new ways to increase flexibility at work: number of hours per week, location, rules on vacations, etc. Try to discuss them with your employees and find ways to make your work environment more tunable to fit everyone's needs.

- Seriously commit to reduce the number of mandatory reports, turning them into A3 reports, informal Gemba Walk board revisions or directly eliminating them if you feel that the value they are providing is lower than the cost of maintaining them.

- Review some situations where you feel that the team did not behave as you expected. Discuss with them how you failed to set a context, or what context would have been useful to avoid the situation. Think of ways to set that kind of context in the future.

- Encourage your teams to constantly improve their boards to show more and more relevant information that can lead to better visibility, communication, and coordination both with managers and other teams.

- If you feel like your teams are mature enough, let them self-form. That means that, for the next project, let them divide themselves into teams. For this to be successful, you have to design a clear context, for example, "teams must be cross-functional" and "teams should have no less than five members and no more than nine." You'll find more advice on rules for creating Agile teams in the next chapter. You can hold the right to make small changes in their proposal, but be careful, for if you don't take their advice, you will probably kill the sense of self-organization.

- A first way to involve your people in team composition is to make them participate in the hiring process. Candidates should spend some time with the team, and the team should be given the right to ban anyone if they feel they won't get along with the other team members. Be careful not to hire someone, no matter how talented and experienced he is, if the team feels he won't fit in with them – remember the "no brilliant jerks" rule!

Recommended Readings

Blanchard K, Ridge G (2009) Helping people win at work: a business philosophy called "Don't Mark My Paper Help Me Get an A". FT Press, Upper Saddle River

Blanchard KH, Oncken W, Burrows H (1991) The one minute manager meets the monkey. Quills, New York

Clippinger JH (1999) The biology of business: decoding the natural laws of enterprise. Jossey-Bass, San Francisco

Netflix Culture presentation (available at http://http://www.slideshare.net/reed2001/culture-1798664)

Semler R (2004) The seven day weekend. Random House

Sobek DK, Smalley A (2008) Understanding A3 thinking: a critical component of Toyota's PDCA management system. Productivity Press

Stacey RD (2010) Strategic management and organizational dynamics, the challenge of complexity. FT Press, London

Sutherland J (2010) The roots of scrum. Available at http://jeffsutherland.com/rootsofscrumACCU2010.pdf

Agile Structures: Scaling Agility

6

From Resource Pools to Cross-Functional Teams

The Growing Start-Up Syndrome (Medinilla's Start-Up Syndrome?)

One of the fastest-growing organizational example is the technology-oriented start-up company with a high-growth-rate. The start-up usually begins with a small set of people, maybe as few as two to five cofounders. The nature and potential of this group is considered by venture capital firms as one of the main drives to invest in this company.

So imagine we have four guys trying to build a cool Internet start-up, and they are doing well. Pretty well, in fact: one of them is the business guy, and he is selling the concept to early clients. We also have a tech guy, who is coding the thing, and a graphical designer who is doing all the look-and-feel stuff. Then, we have a guy taking care of finances and talking to investors, and the four of them are collaborating very effectively: the business guy will give feedback to the tech and graph guys, who will ask the finance guy for more resources. They are a cross-functional, self-organizing, self-managing team, and the magic is happening.

As they start to succeed and get some money from investors and early clients, they'll have more work to do, so maybe the tech guy will hire some coders. When eight coders are developing, the graph guy won't be able to cope with all the requests for icons, graphics, and look-and-feel changes. Maybe he will also realize he will need people with knowledge of user experience issues. So we will hire a couple of guys.

Á. Medinilla, *Agile Management*, DOI 10.1007/978-3-642-28909-5_6,
© Springer-Verlag Berlin Heidelberg 2012

The business guy himself will be overcrowded with meetings, so he will hire some sales guys. Maybe he will also realize that he is not doing as much marketing as he should, and a VP of marketing will also join the management board.

Now, we have 20-something people on board, and the finance guy is drowning in payroll, purchase orders, checks, invoices, etc. He will also start to hire clerks. In the meantime, maybe the new VP is not going along very well with the graph guy because he feels like the look and feel of the application should be supervised by marketing, as it affects customer perception of the product, and the tech guy is maybe creating three different groups of tech people for network, systems, and software, each with a group leader who helps him supervise his growing staff.

All of a sudden, we have 200 people and the original magic of the founding team is gone. Everyone is so busy managing his own people that instead of holding hands and looking to the front, they've turned around and started to look at their own matters instead. Departments are created as isolated responsibility areas with their own line of command, the urge for clients and resources is gone now that we are B-I-I-I-G, and what once was a value-creating Lean machine is now another bureaucratic company in the market, not different from the other niche players.

As some parents would say looking at their punk child, where did we go wrong?

By the way, as it happened with Medinilla's principle of motivation, I'm not aware of any specific literature covering this issue, so I'll try to call it Medinilla's start-up syndrome and see what happens. . .

The Communication-Paths Problem: $n(n-1)/2$

One of the main reasons for the start-up syndrome is that the number of available communication paths in a group of people grows according to $n*(n-1)/2$, where n is the number of persons in the group.[1] That means that it follows an exponential curve related to n^2.

For instance, when you have the original group of four people, you have $4*(4-1)/2 = 6$ available communication paths, as you see in this graph:

---

[1] As we will see later, this idea was originally proposed by F.P. Brooks in his book *The Mythical Man-Month*.

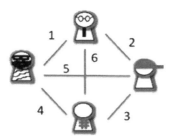

On the other hand, when we grow to 20 people, the number of available communication paths is as large as $20*(20-1)/2 = 190$ communication channels. Who can manage that?

Not the average human being. Early works on the brain's capacity by cognitive psychologist George A. Miller[2] show that the average human brain can hold seven-plus-minus-two chunks of information on what is called in cognitive psychology and neuroscience "the working memory": a system to hold short-term memory information for goal-oriented processing. This could explain why all time-management systems recommend some kind of immediate long-term storage – a list, notebook, index card system, or software tool – of the things you must remember to do, as trying to remember more than seven-plus-minus-two things at the same time will be a source of both stress and forgotten items. It could also explain why most Agile experts agree on an optimal team size of seven plus minus two, meaning 5 to 9 people. If you fall below the "5" mark, you may fall short of skills and critical mass for the magic to happen, but if you go over 9, you start to have communication issues and small mini-teams start to form inside the team.

These mini-teams, if not managed, will be formed many times by affinity, so testers will tribe with testers and coders will join other coders. Traditional organizations mimic this behavior in the form of departments or, as we Agilists like to call them, "knowledge silos."

Knowledge silos are evil.

The first consequence of knowledge silos is that they will increase handoffs and will call for a *waterfallish* way of doing things. That means that, when a work request comes, it will first be routed to the business

---

[2] Miller GA (1956) The magical number seven plus or minus two: some limits on our capacity for processing information. Psychol Rev 63(2):81–97.

analysts, who will then hand it out to the system analyst, who will pass it to the software developers, who will hand it to the testers, who will then pass it to system engineers, who will finally pass it to customer acceptance.

Every handoff introduces delays and inefficiency. What's worse: each step of the waterfall process will have a limited view of the overall process. Coders will not care about the problems system engineers will have while deploying the code, as doing so will increase their work and the time they spend with it. So they will just send some garbage downstairs very, very fast, and when software engineers complain about how difficult it is to deploy the code, they will reply, "that's none of our business, pal! Go earn your paycheck!"

Of course, system engineers can refuse to deploy the code and send it back to developers. But developers may be busy with other requests, so it will take some time until they have a free slot to review their previous code and fix the system development problems. In the meantime, the customer's clock is ticking... When you try to determine who was responsible for the delay, everyone will finger-point other departmens and spend more time and resources doing blame management.

This is one of the ways that suboptimization can happen when everyone looks only at his own piece of work, at his part of the process. And departments, or knowledge silos, favor the emergence of such behavior.

But if we can't form teams of more than nine people, and creating departments is evil, how can we manage growth in the company? How can we create more Agile structures?

Programmers Are Not Bricks

Another problem we should be aware of is the trend to create "resource pools" in software development companies. We have already listed this as a motivational anti-pattern, but it has another negative effect on Agile companies, as it introduces new ways of suboptimization and mismanagement.

The underlying assumption under the "resource pool" approach is that programmers are inter-exchangeable pieces – like bricks or bolts. In fact, the definition of "resource" very well matches that underlying idea: resources are usually associated with something expendable, replaceable, or fungible. Managers of a resource pool will toss assignments to any free resource in the pool as the assignments arrive. If the manager receives an assignment whose particularities make it only suitable for a certain resource, because he is the only one with a particular skill or experience, he will command that resource to take care of the incoming assignment immediately and handle his half-finished current assignment to any other available resource in the pool.

This, of course, is a very inefficient way of managing a software company. And of course, calling your people "resources" is not helping at all. Agile environments need the right people at the right place, and not just the available people. Tom De Marco, in his book *Slack*, has a story about someone looking for a lost needle in a haystack, and some other guy telling him that it is much easier to look for the hay lost in the needle-stack, which is obviously true but absolutely not the point. Here we have a similar situation: the easy way of managing an incoming assignment is to handle it to any available programmer. But if you are in the business of building the next killer application, dominating the market, and making a difference, then getting rid of the assignment as fast as you can is absolutely not the point.

Another appealing concept associated with the "programmers are bricks" paradigm is the Software Factory. The aim of the Software Factory is to apply manufacturing processes to software development through specialization and specific, perfectly defined user requirements and standardized applications. As with software engineering, a concept first proposed in the NATO software engineering conference in 1968,[3] Agile has proven this concept to be an obsolete and archaic way to look at software. Software, we've learned, is complex and unpredictable in ways that make the Software Factory, the resource pool, and software engineering non-suitable approaches to achieve the best possible results.

> "My early metrics book, *Controlling Software Projects: Management, Measurement, and Estimation* (Prentice Hall/Yourdon Press, 1982), played a role in the way many budding software engineers quantified work and planned their projects. In my reflective mood, I'm wondering, was its advice correct at the time, is it still relevant, and do I still believe that metrics are a must for any successful software development effort? My answers are no, no, and no."
>
> –Tom De Marco, *Software Engineering: An Idea Whose Time Has Come and Gone?*

---

[3] Naur P, Randell B (1968) Software engineering: report of a conference sponsored by the NATO Science Committee. NATO Scientific Affairs Division.

Let's look at it from this angle: if you have a group of ten programmers and you take one, how much will productivity decrease? The appealing answer is "ten percent": this will mean that every programmer is doing the same amount of work, for instance, eight programming hours a day. But when you look at high performing teams, you realize that retrieving someone from the group can destroy team dynamics and cut productivity by half or maybe just block the team. What happens if the missing guy is the only analyst or the only tester? What if he is the one creating a fun and collaborating team environment? What if he is the only one who knows about this particular code base and was teaching everyone?

This situation is sometimes seen the other way round: if ten people take 6 months to finish this product, how much time will 20 people need to finish it? Probably, the wrong answer is "three months." As everyone knows, nine pregnant women won't give birth to a baby in 1 month. This fact was noticed as early as 1975 by Fred Brooks in his must-read book, *The Mythical Man-Month*,[4] where Brook's principle, "adding manpower to a late project makes it later," was coined. The explanation, according to Brooks, has to do with the previously discussed communication-paths problem and also with the need of some time for the people joining a project to become productive. This time will actually deduct productivity for other team members, as they will be interrupted with questions, will have to teach and explain things to the newcomers, and will also supervise them and correct their mistakes.

Every today, lots of managers I work with immediately suggest adding more people to projects when they are late, or constantly moving people from one project to another in a sort of "Chinese Spinning Dishes" game where the most critical project gets all the attention, even if that damages another project. The damaged project will of course become 'the most critical project' next week.

Agile's Building Brick: The Cross-Functional Team

The design of Agile structures starts with a simple principle: you don't assign projects to people nor people to projects. You assign projects to teams. Period. If you feel like Michael is the most qualified guy to deal with project Alpha, you will assign project Alpha to Michael's team, set a relative priority and the appropriate context, and let them sort out if Michael

---

[4] Brooks FP (1975) The mythical man-month: essays on software engineering. Addison-Wesley.

is the one who will deal with it or maybe will train someone to do it, so that next time you'll have two available people with knowledge in that area.

The first solution is a short-term approach: make your best engineer take that assignment so you maximize your chances that the project will be on time and on budget. The second one could produce delays and over-cost in the short term, but in the long term, you'll have a better prepared, more robust, and more flexible team. An Agile manager, if possible, will always look for the long-term solution.

Anyway, even for Agile managers, the temptation to consider that "right now" you can't afford to invest in the team's long-term growth and that you will do it "next time" is big. This happens because of how the human brain is hardwired. There is a thing called "instant gratification mechanism" that makes you prone to choose quicker rewards over delayed incentives. That is why diets are so hard: you have to constantly choose between the instant reward of a chocolate doughnut and the future incentive of looking good at the swimming pool, and the average human is not good at this kind of decisions. Shopaholics, compulsive eaters, and other kinds of addicts are other examples of this mechanism in action. On the other hand, studies have shown that the ability in kids to resist instant rewards and delay gratification is associated with higher grades at school and less probabilities of being drug addicted, obese, or divorced in adulthood.[5]

The principle of assigning projects to teams assumes that some team stability is needed. If you are changing team composition every 2 weeks, you are essentially managing a resource pool in disguise. On the other hand, if you are using Agile's definition of a "team," which is more than a group of people commissioned to do the same job, you'll need some time for the team to "glue" or, as some experts call it, "gel together."

In his still-relevant 1965 model of group development,[6] Bruce Tuckman identified four basic stages that any team should inevitably experiment to achieve their maximum performance, and of course this takes some time. If you disband the team every once in a while, you'll have to start from the beginning, or you will always have artificial states of teamwork that don't reach the hyper-productive state we are looking for. Some changes are allowed periodically, of course, as long as you do them gradually taking

---

[5] Casey B J et al (2011) Behavioral and neural correlates of delay of gratification 40 years later. Proc Natl Acad Sci.

[6] Tuckman BW (1965) Development sequence in small groups. Psychol Bull 63 (6):384–399.

care not to destroy the team's identity. The interim between two projects could be a good time to rearrange teams, as long as these projects last for several months – my own rule of thumb is not less than 6 months and not changing more than 10–20% of the team, so you don't experience more than two small team changes a year.

The second principle for growing Agile structures is that you don't grow your organization by making your team bigger, but by making more teams instead. As previously discussed, there are several opinions within the Agile community about the optimal team size, with seven-plus-minus-two being a good place to start, and less than 4 or more than 15 a dangerous land to enter at your own risk.

A suitable way of creating more teams is to keep adding people until you reach a big number, and then split the team into two. The problem with this approach is that it may kill the original team's dynamics and identity. A second way would be to start adding new people until you have five of them trained and then separate these five new members to create their own new team, reverting the first team to its original state. I usually prefer this way.

The third principle for building Agile structures is to create cross-functional teams. There seems to be some confusion in companies I have been coaching about what is the meaning of a cross-functional team, as many people wrongly understand that this is a team where everyone is able to do everything. That's not the idea at all. A cross-functional team, as described in Nonaka and Takeuchi's seminal work, is a group of people where all the skills needed to build an increment of the product are present. That means that we could have one analyst, three coders, two testers, a graphical designer, and a systems expert in the team.

Remember Medinilla's start-up syndrome? The idea behind the cross-functional team is to replicate the original magic that was present when a few people with different backgrounds and skills were constantly interacting, providing feedback, and collaborating to create a killer product end to end – from concept to cash. Once you start to introduce technical or knowledge silos and the consequent handoffs, you create waste and the magic is lost.

About the nature of these cross-functional teams, a general preference for feature teams instead of component or single-function teams can be found in the Agile community. The idea behind a feature team is that they are cross-component enough to develop an end-to-end customer feature, so as feature requests are arriving, you will assign them to available teams. On the other hand, if you have, for example, a specialized team that only does mobile applications and then another team doing web applications, if a web project arrives when the web team is busy and the mobile team is idle, you have a problem.

Component-team defenders are not usually very keen on the idea of specialization either, but they feel that "it's not possible to know about everything." In my opinion, this kind of statements should be enough to under-qualify you as an Agile manager: you are not here to tell us all the things we are not able to do, but to encourage us to learn and grow!

Feature teams have been successfully launched in huge companies like Nokia, Ericsson, or Microsoft. They are building complex products and making these companies more successful, faster, and more customer oriented. How is your product, system, or company more complex than those, up to the point that you can't even consider feature teams? As for different technologies, for example, companies with a Java team and a .NET team, who says that old dogs can't learn new tricks? People will be reluctant to learn different programming languages – sometimes, in fact, they will be reluctant for anything but free beer – but in the long run, it will make them more valuable and will make their team more flexible, robust, and Agile.

Managing Projects Is Not Managing the System

I still have a fourth principle for building Agile structures. This one is called "Orcs at the Gates." In my training seminars, I use this slide to illustrate it:

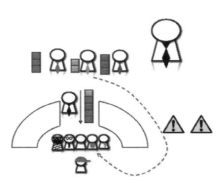

As you can see, there is a cross-functional team at the bottom of the picture. Their problem is that they are working for three different clients, and each of them is asking for immediate attention. As we will discuss in the next chapter, demand will be managed in every iteration, and relative priorities will be set for each customer so he receives a certain amount of the team's capacity in each iteration. The three people with ties at the top of the image can represent clients or maybe internal account managers taking care of one client or project each. The big man in the corner, also wearing a tie, is the manager, while the guy between the clients and the team can be sort of a project manager or team leader.

We can see this situation as an army (the team) that is facing a more powerful enemy (the clients, a.k.a. "the orcs"). If they just try to fight them in the open they will be crushed. But if they find a narrow and protected place where they can make the enemies enter one by one, they can resist. That's what Leonidas and the 300 Spartans did at the Thermopylae and also what the Rohirrim did at Helm's Deep when the army of orcs invaded them (Lord of The Rings, the Two Towers). Orcs in particular are known for not being very intelligent, so they tried to enter through Helm's Deep narrow front door one by one, where the Rohirrim successfully played the "Conga of Death" game for some time.

What I try to show with these metaphors is that the team needs a single entry point of work assignments. If every client is demanding full attention, and even the manager is asking for internal assignments, the team will tend to work on what they think is more important, probably according to who shouts the most or who has more probabilities of firing them, which, of course, is not a good criterion to implement the company's strategy.

Even worse, what happens if a client who gets low attention because of his relative priority makes his way into a merciless team member? As we've learned from history, when Xerxes and the Persians found a mountain track to the rear lines of the Greeks, these where doomed, and so happened with the Rohirrim when the orcs blew part of Helm's Deep wall and entered through the sides.

How do we translate this in the team's situation? If there is a global priority set by the company and suddenly one team member skips that priority to work at something else because he is being pressed to do so, bad things happen. Bad things like delaying more important projects. In the meantime, the account manager responsible for the low-priority project thinks that he is doing a terrific job because he managed to persuade a team member to take care of his project, which, otherwise would have been delayed. But be aware that, in search of his personal goals and agenda, he is playing against the global company goals! Maybe, in the process the most important project is delayed, and that will introduce losses much bigger than the gains of not delaying his low-priority project.

So the question is this: must a team have one and only one person responsible for job assignment and prioritization? The Scrum Agile framework calls him a "product owner," someone who will talk to stakeholders and take the final decision on what is to be built in the next iteration. In some other approaches I have designed, we called this person a "client proxy," a "team's gatekeeper," or even a "project manager," a term that has been banned from many Agile environments because of old negative connotations.

According to my own experience, the Agile manager is usually not a good candidate for product owner. Managing the system is not the same as managing the project, and the product owner is prone to short-term decision making and breaking the "don't assign people to projects" rule when in panic. As we saw in previous chapters, the role of the Agile manager should not be related to job assignment but with defining a system that will automatically route job batches to teams and setting the boundaries, constraints, and goals to make the system work on the most efficient, self-organized, and productive way, as well as helping the system improve. A last reason for the Agile manager not being a good candidate for product owner is that too much power in the product owner's hands will break the balance of power between him and the Scrum Master or Agile coach with bad consequences for the short-term/long-term balance.

What happens then if the manager needs a member of the team to do something for him? My advice would be to put that into the team's backlog and do it through the product owner. I have experienced situations where a whole iteration failed because a manager addressed the only tester in the team and urged him to create a presentation on some topic, so the team couldn't finish the testing of all the stories committed for that iteration. When the manager was blamed for ruining the iteration, he replied, "I didn't know that the tester was so busy! Why did no one tell me?" And he was right in part: the Agile coach and the product owner should have done something. But the fact was that they were so scared of upsetting the manager that they just wished that the whole thing should pass as soon as possible. And the manager was rightly blamed for scaring his people – this is a capital sin for the Agile manager.

The Problem with Specialists

One recurrent problem appears when building Agile cross-functional teams and is that of the hyper-specialist, whose contribution is needed to create a product, but the product will not keep the specialist busy enough to be a full-time member of a team. Graphical designers in not so graphically intense projects or database administrators are typical examples of this. What can we do here?

One approach is to treat them as external suppliers of the teams. The problem with this approach is that coordination and prioritization issues will appear – who should the specialist attend first? – and the specialist will tend to become the bottleneck of the system. This also has the unwanted effect of leaving the specialist out of the team, which can de-motivate him and harm internal networking and collaboration.

Another approach is to create bigger teams: maybe a team of 12 that is managing three or four projects at a time can produce enough work for the specialist to be a full-time member. As he will be sitting with them and attending team meetings, they will be able to self-organize and sort out the best way to set priorities for the specialist.

A third approach that can be combined with the two previous ones is to break the dependency on the specialist. Hyper-specialization is for insects, not for human beings. A long-term program of learning can be instituted so the specialist invests some time training other team members on his craft, until we reach a point where other team members can handle most of the specialist work and still recur to him if there's something difficult that they can't handle on their own. The slack that this introduces for the specialist can be used by him to learn new stuff that widens his knowledge area, so he can join the team as a regular member and not as a specialist anymore.

> "A human being should be able to change a diaper, plan an invasion, butcher a hog, conn a ship, design a building, write a sonnet, balance accounts, build a wall, set a bone, comfort the dying, take orders, give orders, cooperate, act alone, solve equations, analyze a new problem, pitch manure, program a computer, cook a tasty meal, fight efficiently, die gallantly. Specialization is for insects."
>
> –Robert A. Heinlein, *Time Enough for Love*

The specialist sometimes refuses this approach because he feels like being the only one who knows about something gives him power, status, and a sense of safeness (he can't be fired). Of course, no Agile organization will be happy with such a knowledge silo, and the three approaches should be combined to minimize the impact on the system's performance.

The Problem with Support Teams

Another common problem with Agile structures is the support and maintenance of past delivered products. Bugs, new features needed, software updates, and other unpredictable requests will come and interrupt the team's current project, thus introducing context switching, delays, lower performance, and even poorer quality.

An appealing option is to form a support-and-maintenance team that will protect feature teams from interruptions. Well... As valid and popular as this approach can be, I don't like it very much.

The first thing I don't like has to do with motivation. Very few people will enjoy being in a support team – angry customers, broken products, errors, emergencies, outages, crashed servers, etc. Above all, an unpredictable environment where you never know what is going to happen next, and you also never get the chance to build something cool, something that will last, that you can show to others and say "hey, I built this piece of software!"

The second problem is decreased learning. While feature teams are learning new technologies in order to build their products, the support team only learn about them when they break, and then they are in a hurry to fix it, so they don't really have the time to effectively learn about the new framework, tool, or process.

Furthermore, the feature teams and the support team start to be more and more separated, and even if the support team is building some kind of knowledge base where common mistakes and their fix are identified, the feature teams are not likely to be reviewing them, so no stop-the-line-and-fix-the-error-forever is happening: the same mistake will happen over and over in different teams.

Then, we have quality concerns: the feature teams will be less interested in quality, as they will know that if the product breaks, it will be handled by the support team. So they will stop documenting the product and building tests, as they feel like this will slow them down and not benefit themselves but some other team – the support team.

Against these many problems, the only advantage, and it is not a small one, is protection of the feature teams. My own rule for support and maintenance is "everyone eats his own dog food." Teams must support their own code, even if it slows them down. A focus on not repeating the same mistakes and producing as few bugs as possible must be observed at all times, and regular meetings must be held in order to review the state of quality in the team and to plan on how to reduce the technical debt.

One way to manage feature work versus support-maintenance request is to design Scrumban boards, where some capacity of the team will be spared to deal with the average support request rate of the iteration.[7] Other strategies include disbanding the support team and making the former team members join other teams to help them deal with support and maintenance requests.

One special kind of support team is the one that is supporting the rest of the teams on some technical aspect of the development process. Usually, you can find it in the form of a systems team, responsible for maintaining and operating the servers as well as deploying the new products live. My point of view here is the same: the systems team will introduce unnecessary handoffs that the teams should take care of by themselves. Of course, this is more easily said than done, but this cannot be an excuse for the Agile manager not to look for ways to make the system leaner by letting the teams manage their own deploys.

Nevertheless, be careful with an Agile organizational anti-pattern that emerges when you start growing an analyst support team, a testing support team, a graphical design support team, a systems support team and end up with the typical department-based knowledge silo organization!

Free Electrons

As proposed when presenting Lean management, sometimes it is a good investment in the long-term to free your best technical people and let them wander around helping and teaching other teams. I usually call these people "free electrons," and the key for making the most out of them is to keep them absolutely detached from project outcomes and tie their goals only to system improvement and team growth. As soon as they get evaluated for how early

---

[7] You can find information on Scrumban boards in some of my training materials, available at http://slideshare.net/proyectalis

the projects are being delivered, they will lose their long-term sight and start coding like crazy, as they will feel the instant gratification of higher team velocity.

Free electrons can fulfill several roles and team needs. They can be available for teams that need a particular expertise or knowledge, as long as they understand that their duty is not to solve the problem but to show the team how to solve it by themselves next time. They can also focus on an architectural view of the product and provide some insights on architecture in planning and technical meetings, while the teams focus on the short-termed feature they are building.

Another important role of free electrons is to cross-pollinate teams with other team's best practices and lessons learned. If no one cares or invests in showing the best practices to others, improvement opportunities are constrained to the team environment, while other teams will stay at a lower performance level.

Finally, although it is not the main point of free electrons, the fact is that on many occasions, a specially critical project was saved because a special task force of free electrons, your best men, was commissioned to help the project team. This is one of the exceptions noticed by Brooks where adding more people to a late project won't cause the project to be later: if the people added are very knowledgeable on the project, the technology, the team, the product, and the client, then Brook's law may not apply and free electrons may help bring the project back on track.

The Agile Enterprise Model

So now we have four simple rules to build Agile structures:

1. Assign projects to teams, not to persons.
2. Keep teams as stable as possible. Grow by creating more teams.
3. Teams must be cross-functional and should be as feature-oriented as possible.
4. Teams should have one and only one product owner.

These rules are useful for creating teams, and we also have some insights on how to deal with specialists or support teams, but how do we structure several teams together?

There is no clear answer in literature, as every company has its own reality and will produce, or maybe grow, its own Agile structure while following the four basic rules and letting the teams sort out the impediments and problems they find while growing.

In fact, according to my own experience, there is only one main problem that the company must solve when growing Agile structures, and it is the synchronization of different teams and the management of knowledge across them. This need is even more urgent if all the teams are working on the same product, which can lead to cross-dependencies and a higher necessity for coordination.

Companies usually try to institute protocols, processes, forms, reports, and other kind of tools with the aim of synchronizing teams. But the fact is that the best way to do so is through personal interaction, as the Agile Manifesto states as the first value. The same happens with knowledge management: the best, if not the only way to make knowledge effectively travel across teams, is to make people from different teams spend some time together.

Regarding the several teams working in the same project situation, a good practice is to have a regular meeting of product owners to review the product backlog and decide on the priorities for the next iterations and how to divide them between the different teams. This task is easier, of course, if you've succeeded in the creation of feature teams instead of component teams. The more component-oriented the teams are and the more technical the product backlog is, the more you'll need technical architects or experts to attend these meetings and advise the product owners. Sometimes, the figure of a master product owner is appointed to solve any dispute between product owners and take a final decision in case of a tie vote.

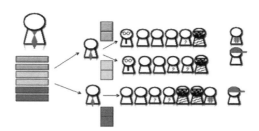

In any case, for teams working on the same project or teams working on different projects, short cross-team meetings in the same format as the daily stand-up held in each team are always worth the effort. Not all members of the team need to attend these meetings, and depending on the degree of dependency between teams, they may not be necessary on a daily basis. A simple team dependencies board, where every team reports what kind of dependencies and problems it is having with other teams, is a good way of managing cross-dependencies: at the end of the cross-team meeting, everyone picks the cards regarding his team and tries to do his best to remove these impediments for other teams.

These kinds of meetings have been recommended by the Scrum Alliance as a best practice under the name of "Scrum of Scrums".[8] The Scrum body of knowledge also proposes a model for scaling them recursively in big organizations with several hundreds of developers in a treelike hierarchy, but Scrum of Scrums or coordination meetings can also be designed as mesh networks, where teams only talk and coordinate with teams they interact with; hub-and-spoke networks, with every team reporting to a central coordination team; or maybe a fully interconnected network, where everyone in the company reports to everyone else. Henrik Kniberg calls this an "all-hands pulse meeting" (Kniberg 2007), and Kanban expert David J. Anderson has reported effective daily meetings with as much as 50 or more people.

> "Kanban daily standup meetings have been shown to be effective with up to 50 or more people. The reason for this is that the team is implicitly trusted to be doing the work that is shown in the visualization of the workflow. There is no need to use the standup to reinforce personal commitment, and hence the standup can focus on the work and not the people. Teams will iterate over the work tickets rather than through the team members. The three questions are obviated. More mature Kanban teams reduce discussion only to work that is impeded or defective, focusing only on exceptions rather than work that is proceeding normally."
>
> –David J. Anderson, "Thoughts on how Kanban differs from Scrum"

Another suitable approach for team coordination is to create an Agile implementation team formed with Agile coaches, managers, product owners, and free electrons: they can take care of the Agile implementation and cope with dependencies and cross-team issues as well.

---

[8] Sutherland J, Schwaber K (2007) The scrum papers. Available at http://jeffsutherland.com/ScrumPapers.pdf

My last advice for growing Agile structures is to form communities of practice. That means that, as specially skilled people like testers or database administrators will be split among cross-functional teams, a special structure may be needed so they meet regularly to learn and discuss about several issues related to their main area of expertise:

- Standards and policies
- Tools and techniques
- Dependencies between their teams and coordination
- Training
- Research and development
- Interviewing and hiring new candidates
- Managing the relationship with other communities (like analyst vs. testers or coders vs. designers)
- Distributing people on teams

The communities of practice have already been studied in this book as a way to increase learning and networking, but as you see, they can also help the Agile structure grow in a more effective way. Free electrons can also dedicate their time to energize those communities and align their efforts to the coordination needs of the company's team structure.

Summary

In order to grow Agile structures, traditional department-based knowledge silos must be abandoned in favor of cross-functional feature teams. No matter how difficult or even impossible you find it at the beginning of your Agile journey, be sure that every single step you take to approach this new strategy will make your company more effective and productive in the long term.

Cross-functional teams should be designed looking at the whole productive system end to end. Business analyst, graphical designers, coders, testers, and system engineers must join together in the challenge of creating new features iterative and incremental. The need for support and maintenance teams should be reviewed, and if possible, they should be joining the feature teams so the teams give support to their own products.

Specialists should be addressed in a similar way: a long-term program to disseminate their skills and avoid the bottleneck they can become. In Agile environments, hyperspecialists are a problem, and a trend to specialization in certain areas while overlapping knowledge with other team members should be encouraged through pair programming, communities of practice, labs, and other previously discussed methods.

A single entry point of job assignments and priorities must be ensured for every team, and individual commissioning must be stopped: projects, tasks, and jobs must be put in the job queue or product backlog of teams, and they must have some autonomy to decide how, when, and who should engage them. Scrumban boards can help to manage and report such decisions.

Cross-team coordination can be achieved through a product owner team that decides on job assignments and feature priorities, as well as Scrum-of-Scrums-like meetings, Agile implementation teams, free electrons, or communities of practice.

Things to Try

- Identify the situations in your company where tasks are commissioned to specific individuals. Debate with the team what effect it has on the team's performance and velocity, and try to design a procedure to route these assignments through a single entry point, probably the product owner or maybe a backlog column on the team's Kanban board.

- Research online for Alexandre Magno's "Executive Scrum" approach. He is using Agile team practices to coordinate the management board as a cross-functional team oriented to value creation. From the "Medinilla's start-up syndrome" perspective, he is regaining the original magic of the start-up team at the top management level.

- Teach your team members not to accept any kind of job assignment if it hasn't passed through their product owner. The product owner should remain accountable for the information on all the work the team is performing, project-related or not. If the team is not reporting the job they are doing or is accepting assignments that do not come through its product owner, the Agile coach should take care of the issue.

- Research on Scrumban boards. You can start with my own presentations on http://slideshare.net/proyectalis. Ask your teams to trace on their Scrumban board not only project-related work but all kinds of support, maintenance, and other kinds of assignments they are receiving.

- Schedule an all-hands monthly meeting. Ask every team to prepare a short 1-min report on what are they working on and the main impediments or issues that they have with other teams. Commit yourself to help and work on the reported issues. In following all-hands meetings, report on the improvements you've accomplished.

- Try to create some free electrons in your organization. If the "free electron" job title is something your organization would not accept, you can appoint technical architects, technical leads, community leaders, or coordination managers. Discuss with them and the Agile coaches how to set improvement, learning, and coordination goals for themselves, and make sure that they are detached from actual project results – those are product owner's goals.

- Create a team-dependencies board where everyone can see it. Make sure to review it frequently and be careful with teams reporting no dependencies, impediment, or issues – they may be hidden.

- Make job titles more flat and wide. Instead of having "database administrators" and "user experience specialists," who will refuse to do things not related to their job description, try to have as many "team members" as possible. Don't try to perfectly define the tasks and responsibilities of every job title – that is Taylorism! Instead, ask every "team member" to use all their skills to help the team succeed in the way they feel will better serve the other team members, and to care about learning and improving year after year.

Recommended Readings

Coplien JO, Harrison NB (2004) Organizational patterns of Agile software development. Prentice Hall, Upper Saddle River

Kniberg H (2007) Scrum and XP from the trenches. lulu.com. (Also available on-line at http://www.infoq.com/minibooks/ scrum-xp-from-the-trenches)

Largman C, Vodde B (2008) Scaling lean & Agile development: thinking and organizational tools for large-scale scrum. Addison-Wesley Professional, Upper Saddle River

Largman C, Vodde B (2010) Practices for scaling lean & Agile development. Addison-Wesley Professional, Boston

Schwaber K (2007) The enterprise and scrum. Microsoft Press, Redmond

Shalloway A, Beaver G, Trott JR (2009) Lean-Agile software development: achieving enterprise agility. Addison-Wesley Professional, Reading

Managing Capacity and Workload

7

Or How to Finally Acknowledge that You Can't Fight the Universe

Managers and Workload

From my own perspective, Agile managers shouldn't be the ones caring the most about workload and team capacity, especially in the short term. If we use Scrum terminology, that is the product owner's role. Managers should give some guidance about operational and strategic priorities, maybe in the form of resources to use for each project or relative importance. But when managers start to arbitrarily set deadlines, scopes, and budgets without consulting the team or the product owner, very bad things happen.

The urge to know about team's capacity, when projects are supposed to be delivered, expected delays, and final scope contents of next releases is too pressing to be resisted most of the time. Furthermore, the temptation to push some last-minute requirement to the team in order to please your client, or maybe your top management, and tell them to "just do it!" will also be very appealing, as they will very seldom fight back, especially if we are talking about teams that have been living a Taylor-Ford culture for a long time and are new to the details of Agile.

On the other hand, with successful Agile implementations at the team level, I very often find desperate managers telling me "they were supposed to deliver in December, and now they say that it's not going to be done before February! And I am not supposed to interfere! Isn't this Agile thing killing us?"

Then we have the first-impression shock of some Agile implementations: when you stop counting work-hours per week[1] and you start focusing on

---

[1] Let me guess, is everyone reporting 40 h of work-related stuff per week? I have bad news for you.

Á. Medinilla, *Agile Management*, DOI 10.1007/978-3-642-28909-5_7,
© Springer-Verlag Berlin Heidelberg 2012

delivered value, maybe you'll realize how few things you are accomplishing. And then fear will strike management, who will irrationally want to go back to the old days, where they didn't feel so uncomfortable about what they were finding out.

Unfortunately, for them, one of the characteristics of a Kaizen or continuous improvement environment is "a perpetual state of discomfort." And I promise you a whole lot of it while following the Agile path.

The fact is probably that you were not that good before Agile. On a few occasions, I've found someone who was in absolute denial and stated that they *never* had any kind of delays before Agile and that *all* projects were delivered on time and on budget. As you can imagine, this was plainly not true and was just the reaction of laggards to a change in status quo.

What's worse: some people I have met claimed that, before Agile, if a deadline was to be met, people would drop vacations, weekends, and even work nighttime until the project was ready and that now they don't see "that kind of commitment."

The truth is that, of course, you had several project delays before Agile. Usually they were hidden by unpaid overtime, which was introduced by fear and managerial pressure and was, of course, killing both motivation and product quality: even the most Tayloristic manager will have to admit that the quality of products coded on a Saturday night after 45 h of continuous coding won't be very reliable.

This unwanted and pernicious situation is creating vicious cycles in ways many companies fail to see. Continuous pressure and hurry make people deliver low-quality code as long as it is working – more or less. This introduces bugs and errors that will have to be handled in the future, thus reducing productivity through support time and context switching. The reduced productivity will delay projects, which will again introduce hurry and pressure, thus closing the circle. But it does not stop there: the low quality of products will make clients angry, introducing more pressure into the circle, and we will even lose some clients, which will reduce profit. Profits will also be reduced because of low productivity, and low profits added to a continuous urgent situation leave no time for developers to train, learn, or invest in reducing the technical debt. This will de-motivate software developers, making them less productive, thus reducing even more the productivity and the quality. And the circle is closed again.

This kind of systemic problem, and not just pushing work into people and pressing team deadlines, is the Agile manager's domain.

The Sales Lunch Syndrome

Sometimes, the problem doesn't come from team managers or product owners but from some other part of the organization, for example, sales. Very often, sales people have goals and bonuses related to the number of sales they make. So, for them, this is the main drive and they won't care that much for other metrics like product quality, project profitability, client satisfaction, returning clients, and churn rate. These will be seen as problems for the production or marketing areas but not for them.

So they will sell just anything, and increasing prices or delaying projected delivery dates will not help them do so. Very frequently I have experienced the situation of a crisis in a project whose deadline was set by the client and the sales guy over a copious business lunch with all sorts of spirituous drinks. When the team was not able to meet that deadline, the sales guy was still seen as a hero by the company, as he was bringing new clients and selling projects, while the team was labeled as "not committed enough" and "incompetent" for not meeting the arbitrary and far-more-than-ambitious deadline.

I have many friends who are sales people: it is a tough and difficult job that requires a lot of unusual skills. I have needed to do it myself when creating my own consulting company, and I have enormous respect for sales people. But many of them will secretly admit that if they push unrealistic deadlines to teams, they sell more and also feel like the team will work harder than if you set a more realistic deadline.

Of course, what we have here again is a problem of suboptimization. As everyone is playing only by their own rules and goals, the game sales people are playing is damaging the ability of the company to perform as a whole. A similar situation led to the subprime mortgage crisis of 2008 and the subsequent market breakdown and global crisis: mortgage sellers were paid according to how many mortgages they sold, and they were not concerned about the reliability of the buyers, their solvency, and if those mortgages were going to be repaid at all or not. The rest is history.

The "sales lunch syndrome" can happen in many other ways. Managers can set arbitrary deadlines according to special market dates (fairs, congresses, client meetings, quarterly reports), or maybe clients themselves will set an unrealistic deadline according to their own needs, and the company will accept it because they fear that if they discuss it, they will lose the contract.

The fact is that the sales lunch syndrome is just another attempt at brute-forcing the system. Try to look at the project from the future: yes, you set a deadline of 6 months; yes, the team accepted the deadline; and yes, 1 month before the deadline the team said that they were not going to make it, and hell was unleashed until the project was delivered on month 9. But if you know that the team did its best during those 9 months, the truth is that it was not possible to deliver the project in 6 months and the mistake was to accept that deadline. If you feel that, looking at it retrospectively, there was a way to deliver the project in 6 months and you didn't realize it, go change your system so the next time you'll take advantage of that strategy. But if your only conclusion is that "the team should have worked harder," "they were not committed enough," or "you needed more resources," you have big chances of brute-forcing the system in a Tayloristic way.

But You Promised!

I have bad news for you: no Agile, Lean, or other kind of method, process, framework, or tool will release you from the responsibility of an adequate customer management. That includes setting a correct context with clients in terms of scope, time, budget, quality, risks, and other project terms and rules for managing the project and dealing with uncertainty, and also managing their expectations.

If you have done your homework, by now you should understand that software development is not a predictive process, so setting a deadline is fine as far as you leave some constraints variable. If you reduce and simplify the project space to scope, budget, and time, that means you can fix one of them, or even two, as long as you leave the other variable. For example, you could set a deadline and a budget and say "by the end of November we will deliver something at this price – but we are not sure if it's going to have 80 or maybe 100 features; what we promise is that it will have at least 80 features, and that those will be the most important on the list."

But if the feature set is fixed, then we have a problem, because fixing a budget, for example, will also fix time, as most of the software development costs are time based. We could fix feature set and time, leaving budget open, and then see if putting enough people into the project can make the deadline feasible – which may be still wrong, as there is a minimum amount of time and money needed to build anything, and putting more people into the project may not reduce the deadline appreciably (remember Brooks' law!). On the other hand, fixing the feature set in advance has proven not to be an advisable way of developing software, as clients are known to define what they actually need when being able to actually use the product.

> "The best way to achieve predictable software development outcomes is to start early, learn constantly, commit late, and deliver fast. This may seem to cut against the grain of conventional project management practice, which is supposed to give more managed, predictable results. But predictability is a funny thing; you cannot build with confidence on a shifting foundation. The problem with conventional approaches is that they assume the foundation is firm; they have little tolerance for change."
>
> –Mary Poppendieck, *Lean Development and the Predictability Paradox*

In fact, I have breaking news for managers: predictability is not the point! Lean managers moved long ago from the market-prevailing paradigm of being able to predict delivery dates, future capacity, and resource needs to a change-and-adapt way of operating, and now they rule their markets. For them, continuous improvement, increasing value, reducing waste, and letting the system flow nonstop are the main targets of their managerial duties.

To reach that state, Lean companies moved from big to small batches of work, thus reducing uncertainty. So maybe reducing the size of your projects is a good way to start coping with deadlines and predictability. Committing to an iteration is easy and holds a controlled amount of uncertainty that can be soon determined and used to predict next iterations, while committing to a 12-month-long project will very probably move uncertainty as close to the deadline as possible, making it impossible to steer the project when we find out that the original estimates were too optimistic or unrealistic.

Seeing how complex the predictability of software project is, it seems like someone using the "we promised!" argument to steer a project is being unreasonable, non-educated, and childish. It reminds me of the typical conversation that parents have with kids, where they will say, "look son,

I know I promised to take you to the amusement park, but it's raining badly," and the kid replies, "but you promised!." In this case, the father failed to set the context: "I promise that, if weather and other circumstances allow it, I'll take you to the amusement park." And the process to follow if the circumstances were adverse was not set either.

Yes, clients will complain when a deadline is not going to be met. But brute-forcing the system, as we've seen, is not an Agile option. Be prepared to explain in detail the reasons for the delay, as if they are reasonable we should expect the client to understand them, especially if you provide a way to deal with changes and have something to deliver on the promised date – even if it does not feature all the promised functionalities.

Anyway, complaining, pressing, and demanding is the inherent nature of clients and, as we said before, no method will substitute a good client management approach.

The Two Good Moves and the Three Bad Moves in Pipeline Management

Let's try to simplify demand and see it as an incoming pipeline of small batches of work (features, for instance) that are prioritized and assigned to the team, as in this graphic:

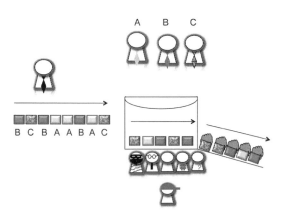

In order to use a pipeline approach to portfolio management, you must be sure first that you have feature-cross-functional teams, so every batch of work is self-contained and can be delivered by any team as "working software" at the end of an iteration. You must also have capable product owners who know how to break big requests in small batches that can be independently scheduled in a determined order. If that is the case, maybe you can use a Kanban approach for your whole portfolio management, creating a "Backlog" column and a "Selected for Next Iteration" column, where the next features to be developed will be always specified.

Considering all this, if you have an average velocity of five features per iteration, and as long as the product owner is doing a good job dividing projects in similar-sized batches, you can have a fairly good predictability on when each feature of the backlog is supposed to be delivered and also update that information frequently according to the team velocity measured at the end of every iteration.

Now imagine that the first client, A, has an urgent request of three features. What can the product owner do? Well, for me, he has five options: two of them are good, two are bad, and one final option is directly dangerous.

The first good move he could make is to accept the request, put it at the end of the queue, and promise the client that as soon as there is some available space in a still-noncommitted iteration, his three features will be the first to be scheduled. Of course, when I tell product owners or sales people to do this, they look at me incredulously as if I'm mad. I can't understand why, as this is, most of the time, the best thing you could do. Everything in the pipeline was a priority several days ago, so now that today's priority arrives, do the former stop being priorities? Even worse, if we delay the whole pipeline to attend this new urgent request, we won't be able to deliver other features on the promised deadlines.

What we experience here, again, is a case of instant-reward versus delayed gratification. The product owner prefers the instant reward of a happy customer instead of discussing, arguing, and explaining that he can't just stop everything every time the client feels the urgency of an unpredicted need. About the other delayed features, well, we will see that in options number four and five.

Sometimes, nevertheless, the three urgent unpredicted features will in fact be urgent, and there won't be an option to put them at the end of the queue. Then, and only then, should we play option number two: delay all client A's features, and put these three new features instead. Looking at the graphic, that could even mean doing B's feature first and then using the three A slots to deliver these new urgent features, but of course the originally scheduled A features will be delayed in favor of the new ones.

As rational as this may seem, many clients will complain and fight back if three of his older requests are delayed in favor of his own three new, more urgent requests. If the product owner is pressed enough, he will probably start to consider nonrational moves, like option number three: put the three incoming urgent requests at the beginning of the pipeline. If he does so, even if he is not telling the clients, the reality is that the whole pipeline will be delayed in three slots. That's not fair, client B and C will definitely agree, as their projects are being delayed because of the need of client A, which is none of their business!

Having reached this point, move number four is practically automatic and has been often discussed in Agile literature: the product owner bursts into the iteration and commands the team to finish the already committed iteration backlog *and* the three new incoming features.

Of course, again, this is a way of irrationally brute-forcing the system by pushing the problem out of his desk. Very often, the team will not be mature enough to say "no," and when they under-deliver, or deliver something that does not work, the old "you promised!" tune will be sung to them.

In iteration-based implementations of Agile, breaking the team's iteration is considered a capital sin: it breaks flow, introduces context switching and reduces team's autonomy and motivation. When this situation is frequent, many teams have moved to a Kanban approach, where priorities can be set and managed in a smaller time frame, even daily. The trade-off is that maybe changing priorities will be encouraged, and planning in the long term will become more difficult.

We still have a fifth move you've maybe guessed: adding more resources! As we've already showed, programmers are not building blocks, and adding more resources in the short term is more likely to increase costs and delay the project even more rather than to improve anything.

The Two Golden Principles in Portfolio Management

For better or worse, the truth is that portfolio management does not have more complex rules than the ones we've already discussed in the pipeline example. Agile companies manage their portfolio by creating a backlog of pending features or work batches, sometimes in the form of "epics" or group of features. They prioritize them, give some kind of rough high-level estimation of effort needed, and then decide on the top priorities to be addressed during next iterations. And then, they repeat the process constantly and frequently.

Anyway, there are two basic principles that, hard as they are to follow, will help you to better manage your portfolio:

1. *Trying to please everyone is the sure path to mediocrity.* I think I got this phrase from a similar one used by Colin Powell. He used it in a leadership sense, meaning that if you avoid the tough decisions, confronting who needs to be confronted, and prioritizing some things over others, you'll miss the best results you can get and settle for "good enough" instead.

> "I don't know the key to success but the key to failure is to try to please everyone."
>
> —Bill Cosby
>
> "If I had asked people what they wanted, they would have said faster horses."
>
> —Henry Ford
>
> "You can't just ask customers what they want and then try to give that to them. By the time you get it built, they'll want something new."
>
> —Steve Jobs

2. *If you can't say "no," your "yes" means nothing.* I heard this phrase from Esther Derby on XP 2011 and decided to use it as a way to explain principle number two instead of the one I was using until then: "focusing and effective prioritization means learning how to say 'no' to everything but what you are doing right now." Ironically, trying to please all your clients by saying "yes" to anything they ask for will, ultimately, make them mad at you, because you can't please everyone at the same time.

> "Have the courage to say no. Have the courage to face the truth. Do the right thing because it is right. These are the magic keys to living your life with integrity."
>
> —W. Clement Stone
>
> "Half of the troubles of this life can be traced to saying yes too quickly and not saying no soon enough."
>
> —Josh Billings
>
> "All the mistakes I ever made were when I wanted to say 'No' and said 'Yes.'"
>
> —Moss Hart

Handling the project portfolio is a matter of selecting what to work at next, always considering that, as we will see next, a healthy backlog has more things than those that the company can handle before a given date. Criteria used to prioritize the backlog should mix short- and long-term concerns, including company strategy, market opportunities, available resources, project risks, etc. In that decision, a few projects, epics, client requests, or individual features will be chosen to configure the next iteration, but if we keep changing those priorities every time clients are upset, we will make the situation worse introducing waste, context switching, lower productivity, decreased morale, poor quality, and, ultimately, building a technical debt monster that will eat your company for breakfast.

Sisyphus, the First Product Owner

In many cases, Agile will provide simple and valuable measures on team capacity that will let you realize that you have more work to do than the capacity to do it! Is it time for the product owner to panic?

This always reminds me of Sisyphus. As you probably know, Sisyphus is a character from Greek mythology who was punished to roll a huge rock up a hill, only to watch it roll back down every day. For me, this is a good image to depicture the product owner versus team's capacity.

Product owner sees a team capacity of 10 average features per iteration, and he sees that if they were able to do 12, they would be on time for every project. So the team strives for improvement, investing in reducing technical debt, learning new skills, implementing better tools and practices, etc. And some months later, they are able to do 12 average features per iteration! Woo-hoo! So they live happily ever after, right?

As you have already imagined: wrong. As the team now has higher capacity, the company will be pushing more work to them. So now that the team has a velocity of 12, probably the product owner wishes that the capacity was 14 so they could make every project successful. And thus, the product owner is punished to roll the team's capacity rock up the portfolio hill, only to see how the portfolio always grows beyond the team's capacity.

The fact is that healthy companies have *slightly* more work to do than the capacity to do it. If this is not the case, the company has spare capacity that it is not using, which is a terrible form of waste: the company will need to find more clients and work to do, thus increasing the portfolio, or reducing headcount until capacity matches workload.

If companies have *much more* work than capacity to do it, then the delays will be unacceptable. Ways of dealing with this situation include growing the company, which will take some time, increase costs, and reduce performance because of a bigger complexity; or increase prices, which will make the demand lower while maintaining costs and profits, but will not let the company grow. A mix between both approaches will probably be the most suitable way to deal with a growing portfolio.

If the company has a workload slightly bigger than capacity, a work queue will be formed. This queue will be emptied on low-demand periods, and the most tangible effect will be that projects will not be done immediately, as a small delay will be experienced while queuing. In those cases, trying to do all projects at once will seriously affect lead time, as Kanban systems have proven. A more suitable approach will be to select the next critical projects and perform them nonstop before starting new projects. If nonstop development of projects is considered not possible, this must be seen as a major corporate impediment and addressed through an urgent Kaizen program.

Dealing with Bottlenecks

So you have more work than you can handle, and you want to increase your capacity. The wrong way of doing it would be to ask every single part of your production process or value stream to work harder and produce more, which will inevitably bring inefficiencies through suboptimization. Consider, for example, the following graphic:

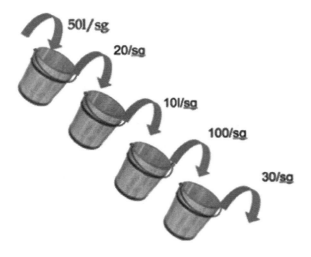

Maybe you will think that this is an oversimplification of productive processes, but I have found this example to be very useful on frequent occasions when trying to explain how to deal with bottlenecks at value streams.

As you see, there is a bottleneck in the second bucket, which is producing a throughput of just 10 l/s. Trying to introduce more work will only lead to water leakage (waste), and the global throughput of the system will still be 10 l/s.

What happens when you ask every bucket to increase performance by 10%?

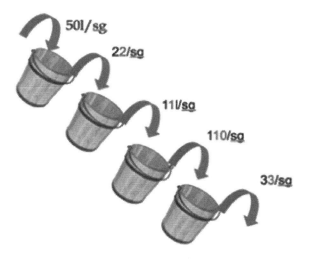

As you see, global throughput has been effectively increased by 10%, from 10 to 11, but the cost has been very high – a total of 16 percentage units have been spent. If those 16 units were used exclusively to raise the bottleneck, we could have increased its throughput to 20 and then use the remaining 6 points between buckets one and two, thus increasing global throughput to 23 – that's a 130% improvement at the same cost! And, by the way, buckets three and four would possibly be much happier than in the first case, where they didn't understand why they were required to increase their throughput with no noticeable results to global performance.

As you see, a good way of increasing your capacity is spotting your main bottleneck and working on it until it is not your bottleneck anymore, then work on the next bottleneck. This is one of the principles behind the Theory of Constraints (ToC). Originally introduced by Eliyahu Goldratt in his 1984 best-selling business novel, *The Goal* (Goldratt 1984), and extended later in his subsequent books *Critical Chain* (Goldratt 1997) and *Theory of Constraints* (Goldratt 1999), ToC focuses on the premise that bottlenecks can be attacked following a systematic process of exploiting, subordinating, and elevating.

Exploiting means that first of all you must make sure that the bottleneck is operating at its maximum capacity. Orders, jobs, and assignments that can be handled by other parts of the system that are not so constrained should be reassigned, so the bottlenecked resource can concentrate on the parts that cannot be performed elsewhere. Jobs should arrive in the best possible condition, so the resource doesn't waste time preparing or rearranging them, and you must make sure that the constrained resource is not blocked or facing impediments at any time, as the whole system will suffer for any delay in the bottleneck.

Once you make sure that the bottleneck has been exploited, it is time to subordinate the system to the constrained resource. In a production line, or a value stream, nobody should work faster than what the bottleneck can handle. If the previous stage of the production line is overloading the bottleneck, that won't make it more efficient – more probably, it will collapse and crash it. When the system subordinates to the bottleneck, it can happen that previous stages of the production process are waiting for the bottleneck to create available slots, while next stages are idle waiting for the bottleneck to provide something to work at – use those free resources to work at the bottleneck! Train them and let the bottleneck delegate some of its duties to the previous and subsequent production stages.

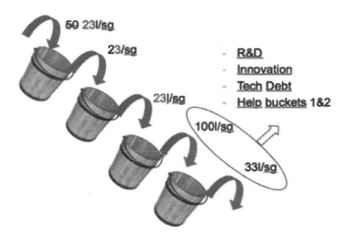

Kanban systems introduce ToC subordination through the use of WIP limits; WIP stands for work in progress. Once the WIP limit has been established for the bottleneck, nobody can produce more work for the bottleneck than the maximum WIP that it allows. If queues or inventories are allowed, arriving assignments that cannot be handled by the bottleneck will start to form a queue that will instantly be visualized on the Kanban board, hence calling for managerial support and decisions on how to deal with the bottleneck.

Finally, if you've exploited the bottleneck, subordinated the system, and still you need more capacity, you can elevate the bottleneck, meaning that you can add more resources to the system. Remember Brooks' law anyway: the elevation will take place in the long term, not for the current project, which is more likely to experiment further delay because of the elevation process.

Metrics for Capacity

I would like to end this chapter by briefly introducing some ways that Agile teams use to measure capacity.

First, you have the good-ol' man-hour. I must admit that I have personal issues with the man-hours, as I always see them as a vestigial defect from Taylor's age, but to be honest, most Agile teams I've known – and I've known them by the hundreds – are still using man-hours to measure their capacity (which does not mean that *the best* Agile teams are using them).

If you use man-hours, there's a trap you must avoid, which is to count the people in your team, multiply for 40 h a week, apply some kind of arbitrary focus factor – time that you ask them to focus on the project – and end up with a number that you will measure them against. If you do that, I predict constant delays and frustration, followed by a lack of trust from management.

The first reason is that teams are not perfect machines. They have good weeks and bad weeks – full of interruptions, priority changes, reports, meetings, mandatory trainings, rework, bugs, etc. They face easy features and features from hell. And they have days when they are creative and innovative, and days when their whole code should be rewritten or directly thrown into the bin.

Managers will tend to take the best-week capacity and say "see? When you work hard, this is what you can accomplish." And then plan their projects counting that capacity for *every week*. Which of course won't happen: hence the delay and the lack of trust.

Instead of calculating a "wanna-have" capacity, you should look at the team's historical data and obtain an average, as well as a maximum capacity and a minimum capacity. With those numbers and some estimation for the backlog, you can provide three important predictions: the minimum time to deliver (using your maximum capacity), the maximum time to deliver (using your minimum capacity), and the expected delivery time (using the average). These three numbers will form a bell curve of probable delivery dates, with the biggest area around the expected delivery time and a certain trend to move to the maximum delivery time, as in this graphic – which I usually call "Medinilla's Law of Project Unfairness" because projects can be earlier to a certain degree but can be late almost unlimitedly.

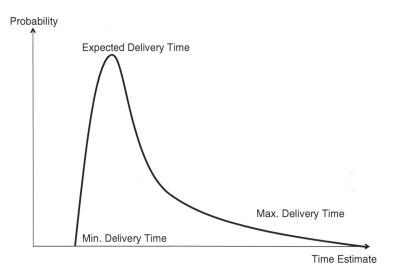

Anyway, as I said before, I don't like to use man-hours. If you drop the artificial habit of forging the wanted capacity using number of people and multiplying by hours, then it is easier to move to average features or, as Agilists usually refer to them, story points.

But first, let me make a case against man-hours:

- If I work 8 hours today and you work 8 hours, are we producing the same?
- If this product has 1,500 man-hours in it and this other similar product has 1,500 man-hours too, have they got the same number of features? The same quality?

- If I say that I can do this feature in 6 hours and you say 12, is one of us wrong? What estimate should we assign to this feature?
- If 2 years ago I produced 35 hours a week, last year I produced 35 hours a week, and this year I produce 35 hours a week, does that mean that my productivity hasn't changed over the years?
- If a project was estimated in 1,000 man-hours and 500 man-hours have already been invested, is the project half done?

Man-hours are a metric of cost and effort but not a good productivity or capacity metric. So that's why many mature Agile teams move to story points or average features and measure the amount of functionality delivered per iteration. Remember that there is a principle in the Agile Manifesto that reads, "Working software is the primary measure of progress" – this is it!

Once you have some historical data on average functionalities delivered, you can use that average number to make predictions in the midterm, but remember to review those predictions over and over in each iteration, as while you progress on your project you will reduce uncertainty and the bell curve will be more and more precise.

Summary

Managing capacity in a software company is not just a matter of setting deadlines, flogging the team through the project, and asking everyone to increase their capacity. Agile companies are learning better and simpler ways to manage the project portfolio by building corporate backlogs, limiting the work in progress to the company's capacity and then working the system to spot and improve existing bottlenecks. Kanban and the theory of constraints provide a good way to do it.

Overall, the Agile manager must learn to gently say "no" and stop trying to please everyone, as this will most probably lead to angry clients and mediocre productivity in the long term. Instead, a mechanism of backlog prioritization must be instituted and thoroughly followed.

Studying the average iteration capacity of the team is another way of managing workload in the midterm. Special care must be taken not to arbitrarily set capacity goals but to rely on historical information and relentlessly work the system to improve the average capacity. Using productivity metrics based on value delivered to the client instead of effort-based metrics will help to have the adequate information to manage the backlog efficiently.

Things to Try

- Build a company backlog with all the projects and features already scheduled for the next few months. Make it visible through some kind of portfolio backlog board. Ask all teams to include on the board any assignment they are working on that is not shown there right now, as well as any changes in priorities. Discuss with product owners these changes and assignments and see how they affect already committed deliveries.

- Use the portfolio backlog to start a portfolio Kanban, where you can see pending features, ongoing features, and delivered features. Use it to obtain lead times and cycle time, spot bottlenecks, and trigger discussion on how to improve portfolio management. Remember to limit the work in progress!

- Review the deadline-setting process in your company. Make sure that sales people are evaluated not only by sales but also by the quality and results of those sales.

- Make product owners, not teams, accountable for deadlines. Teams should give estimates for features, and they should maintain, if not improve, average capacity or velocity. Product owners should use that information to estimate deadlines, but if the deadline is not met while the team still maintained its average velocity, make it a product owner's issue, as pressing the team won't help you solve the problem – they are in fact performing as they always have been.

- Work in smaller batches. Make analysts, product owners, teams, and everyone in your organization search for ways to reduce the average feature, task, or work package. The smaller the package, the easier to manage the portfolio, and efficiently steer it when priorities change.

- Make sure that teams are delivering working software at the end of every iteration. The definition of working software should be "as close to live-in-production as possible," and you should have working Kaizen programs to make it even closer to "live," no matter what kind of environment you are working in. Telecom companies usually worked for 6 months to a year before they had something they could put "live," and they are moving fast to shorter 2- or 3-month-like cycles, so you should be seriously considering the same.

- Start measuring team capacity per iteration. Build historical data you can use to better predict next deliveries.

- Always provide three estimations (worse, average, expected) instead of one (deadline), thus giving a measure of the uncertainty of the estimation.

Review the bell curve after every iteration, so client has always the best possible information on the current state of the project and risk of delay.

- Learn and teach your teams how to use story points and play planning poker – you'll find several resources online, and Mike W. Cohn's *Agile Estimating and Planning* is the authorized source (Cohn 2005).

Recommended Readings

Anderson DJ (2003) Agile management for software engineering: applying the theory of constraints for business results. Prentice Hall, Englewood Cliffs

Brooks FP (1975) The mythical man-month: essays on software engineering. Addison-Wesley, Reading

Cohn MW (2004) User stories applied for Agile software development. Addison-Wesley Professional, Reading

Cohn MW (2005) Agile estimating and planning. Prentice Hall, Englewood Cliffs March 11, 2004

Goldratt EM (1984) The goal: a process of ongoing improvement. North River Press, Croton-on-Hudson

Goldratt EM (1997) Critical chain. North River Press, Croton-on-Hudson

Goldratt EM (1999) Theory of constraints. North River Press, New York

Krebs J (2008) Agile portfolio management. Microsoft Press, Redmond

Agile Culture and Driving Change

From Dilbert to Googlers

8

First Who, Then What

In his 2001 book, *Good to Great* (Collins 2001), American business consultant Jim Collins presented a research done on 1,435 good and profitable companies over 40 years, trying to find those that systematically beat the average good companies, and found 11 companies that exceeded their industry's average results by at least three times – the average being 6.9 times greater than their market's average – and they did it over 15 years in a row. Pretty impressive, if you ask me.

When he looked for common patterns in those companies, what he found was not in the line of superior technology, better-prepared employees, right processes, high salaries and bonuses, or big change programs. In fact, seven common patterns were identified, three of them being:

- "Level 5" leaders who are humble and committed to do what's best for the company
- Getting the right people on board and letting them find the best position and role they can perform
- A culture of discipline and commitment to excellence

This is an important message worth considering: if you have the right people, the right culture, and the right leadership, you have big chances of succeeding, while if you have wrong people, culture, and leadership, other facts may not matter at all: the best you should expect is average performance and mediocre products. Remember Medinilla's principle of motivation, "no de-motivated team has ever changed the world." Well, the same happens with corporate cultures.

Á. Medinilla, *Agile Management*, DOI 10.1007/978-3-642-28909-5_8,
© Springer-Verlag Berlin Heidelberg 2012

> "Organization doesn't really accomplish anything. Plans don't accomplish anything, either. Theories of management don't much matter. Endeavours succeed or fail because of the people involved. Only by attracting the best people will you accomplish great deeds."
>
> –Colin Powell, "Colin Powell's 18 Leadership Principles"

If you've read this whole book to this point, you may have noticed how I love principles. Principles differ from laws and theories in being truths we accept through direct observation, instead of mathematical demonstrations or exploratory statements. So here is another principle for you: different people will perform differently in different corporate cultures – Medinilla's Corporate Cultures Principle.[1]

Again, it is a matter of the right people in the right culture. But what comes first? According to Collins, it starts with who gets on the bus and then you can let them decide where to drive it – first who and then what.

What Corporate Culture Is and Is Not

It is easy to say that "people are your most important assets" and then print some cool values and principles in the lobby, but leaders who really "walk the talk" and nurture a great corporate culture are the ones who make the difference.

What is a corporate culture anyway? In his pioneer works about organizational culture and leadership, Edgard H. Schein defines it as "A pattern of shared basic assumptions invented, discovered, or developed by a given group as it learns to cope with its problems of external adaptation and internal integration."[2] It is not much different from the Merriam-Webster definition of culture, "the integrated pattern of human knowledge, belief, and behavior that depends upon the capacity for learning and transmitting knowledge to succeeding generations."

Don't complicate yourself: corporate culture is "the way we do things around here."

---

[1] OK, that's it, no more "Medinilla principle" jokes.

[2] Shein E (1985) Organizational culture and leadership: a dynamic view. Jossey-Bass.

Schein identified three layers that define corporate culture: the first layer is composed by artifacts – any tangible or verbally identifiable elements of the organization. How people dress, verbal expressions only used by them, the kind of furniture or gadgets they have around, and other physical and verbal elements can identify and influence corporate culture. In fact, people in strong corporate cultures are often described as "tribal" or even "sectarian" by those outside of the culture, who will clearly identify it and notice the strong adherence of the people to it.

Consider, for example, Googlers, as Google employees call themselves. Googlers are a common example of a strong and easily identifiable corporate culture. They are prone to exhibit Google stuff, like t-shirts, badges, baseball caps, or other corporate signs, and they also spend a lot of time with other Googlers, both at the company and outside. Google actively invests in its own cultural artifacts, as you can check if you search for some of the multiple presentations about their office style (Google Zurich offices are specially impressive!).

"Bad" corporate cultures can also be identified through artifacts – physical and verbal elements. Cultures of "if it ain't broken don't fix it," "you are not paid to think," or "that's not my job/my fault," for instance. Or cultures of staying late at the office so the manager doesn't get angry at you, sending lots of e-mails to seem busy and productive, cursing and shouting regularly at each other, or scheduling endless meetings – "the way things work around here." You can even spot them through physical objects as surveillance cameras, control forms, strict dress codes, or Big Brother-style posters and signs.

Can you see why the term "tribal" is used? The tribe resides in the collective mind, as a representation of what "us" means, and shared physical, verbal, and behavioral signs are a way to enhance and develop tribal identity, as it is to share common ceremonies, goals, events, etc. In fact, some sociologists have proposed that, with the loss of the sense of traditional tribes in modern societies, people are looking for those bounds at workplaces. Most psychologists also agree that our "self," our identity, is strongly influenced – if not forged – by the culture we are experiencing.

Going back to Schein's model, his second layer of corporate culture is composed of espoused values. These are the values actively pursued by the company and communicated by the management. But the real values, those by which employees actually live for and are integrated in office dynamics, constitute Schein's third cultural layer, what he calls assumptions.

Of course, if there is misalignment – or even conflict – between espoused values and assumptions, the corporate culture will fail.

Researchers of corporate culture have made clear the difference between espoused values and assumptions, up to the point that most of them nowadays consider that values communicated by the management are not a part of corporate culture unless they are first aligned with real values, those that employees really care for and will put before everything. You can look at this alignment from both sides: the alignment between management's message and the correct set of employees who will react to that message, and the alignment between a given set of employees and a manager who will create a message that will make them react.

> "Lots of companies have nice sounding value statements displayed in the lobby, such as: Integrity, Communication, Respect, Excellence...
>
> Enron, whose leaders went to jail, and which went bankrupt from fraud, had these values displayed in their lobby: Integrity, Communication, Respect, Excellence. These values were not, however, what was really valued at Enron
>
> The actual company values, as opposed to the nice-sounding values, are shown by who gets rewarded, promoted, or let go. Actual company values are the behaviors and skills that are valued in fellow employees. At Netflix, we particularly value the following nine behaviors and skills in our colleagues, meaning we hire and promote people who demonstrate these nine."
>
> –Netflix Corporate Culture presentation

In his 10-year, 24,000-person organizational research study, the authors of *Tribal Leadership* (Logan et al. 2008) identified two main elements to define corporate culture: core values and a noble cause. The values will be aligned with Schein's idea of espoused values and assumptions, while the noble cause introduces a new factor of alignment, commitment, and corporate identity. The noble cause is described in terms of defining a future state that is to be achieved through the tribe's coordination: it is what the tribe shoots for, what it is in service of.

As with espoused values and assumptions, if the management's noble cause – or purpose, or vision, if we use the motivational terms shown in Chap. 4 – differs from the aims of the people who form the culture, then a dissonance will occur that will break the desired corporate culture. On the other hand, as you remember from Chap. 4, even if management and employees are aligned in their cause, if it is not a noble one, you can end up with the Third Reich – be sure that you care enough about the noble cause definition for your corporate culture.

Tribal Leadership authors conclude in their studies that leaders should not impose values and a noble cause but instead engage their people – the tribe – in an exploratory process of what the tribe stands for (values) and what it lives for (noble cause), and then ensure that all behaviors in the company are in line with them. A tribal leader will protect the tribe's identity.

Smell of WOWness: Zappos and Corporate Culture

We've already shown many companies with strong corporate cultures in this book, like Semco, Netflix, or Google. American online shoe retailer Zappos, who achieved one billion dollars in gross merchandise sales in 2008 and was acquired in 2009 by Amazon in an all-stock deal worth about $1.2 billion, is another example of what can happen when a strong corporate culture is enforced and embraced.

Their story has been published by Zappos CEO Tony Hsieh in his book *Delivering Happiness* (Hsieh 2010), and their corporate culture has been codified in the *Zappos Culture Book*, which is created by all Zappos employees by sharing unedited stories about what they value and what they don't at their workplace.[3] They even have a website where they discuss their culture, zapposinsights.com, and they've launched seminars for managers and leaders of other companies who want to learn how to create such an environment in their workplaces.

Let's try to briefly describe Zappos culture: it starts with the interviewing process, where an assessment of personality and culture fit will be conducted. No matter how talented a candidate is, he will not be hired if he is not a good fit for Zappos culture. All new hired employees, including managers, are required to go through a 4-week customer-loyalty training course that includes 2 weeks of taking direct customer calls. After those weeks, all new employees are offered $2,000 to quit, no questions asked – only 3% take the deal.

---

[3] It is freely available for everyone who asks for it – worldwide.

Zappos offices are something to study. They share some Google-style goodies, like free lunch and snacks, playrooms with videogames, or a nap room, but when you read that some departments have decorated their whole place to look like a jungle – or used an Elvis-themed decoration – and that the CEO's desk, in the middle of nowhere, has an inflatable monkey hanging from lianas, then you start wondering if these guys are plain crazy or are into something different and revolutionary.[4]

The reason for this crazy office environment is that, when asked to identify ten core values, Zappos employees chose "Create Fun and A Little Weirdness" as one of them. And, as we already explained in Chap. 4, they feel like their office is not their product. Many managers I have discussed this case with would express their concern that clients visiting the office would find their behavior nonprofessional, which would damage the company. But ironically, what Zappos is experiencing is exactly the opposite: clients are queuing and even paying to make a tour around Zappos offices!

Zappos culture encourages client service over everything. For them, giving good service is not enough: they want their clients to be amused, or, as they call it, "deliver WOW through service." Many companies will claim the same ("we must deliver superior customer service") and then make their clients go through impersonal and inefficient call robots and urge their call agents to terminate calls as fast as possible in order to increase "productivity." They will also force the agents to use pre-engineered scripts to handle calls and be more "efficient," and calls will be frequently monitored by supervisors to enforce the company's policy.

This would be a clear case of conflict between espoused values and assumptions and also of Taylorism applied to customer service. But Zappos is not doing that. The management message and the real values are aligned, so all behaviors are consequent with it: there are no scripts nor limits to call times, the longest call recorded exceeding 5 hours. They even have call agents working from home, something that goes against the common practices of the call-center industry.

The results of effectively sustaining this customer-centric culture are stunning. Zappos customer service consistently ranks as one of the best in the USA, has been compared to those of Jaguar or Ritz Carlton, and considered superior to the ones provided by BMW, Cadillac, or Apple.

---

[4] Tip: remember their stock market value and gross merchandise sales.

When you ask Zappos' CEO about their results, he would just answer that it all starts and ends with corporate culture: if the culture is right, people will do the right thing.

"From the outside, the first company, LinkExchange, that I co-founded seemed like a success. It was actually a pretty sad thing selling the company. Most people don't actually know the reason why we ended up selling the company. It's because the company culture just went completely downhill. I remember when it was just five or 10 of us; it was kind of like your typical dot-com back in the day. This was 1996, and we were working around the clock, sleeping under a desk, had no idea what day of the week it was, but it was a lot of fun. But we didn't know any better to pay attention to company culture.

So, by the time we got to 100 people, we hired all the people with the right skill sets and experiences, but not all of them were culture fits. And when we got to 100 people, I remember I myself dreaded getting out of bed in the morning to go to the office. And that was kind of a weird feeling because this was a company that I co-founded and if I felt that way, then I wondered how all the other employees must have felt.

So, we ended up selling the company. And with Zappos I wanted to make sure that I didn't make the same mistake again. So from the beginning culture has always been really important and to this day, culture is actually the number one priority in the company. And our whole belief is that if we get the culture right, then most of the other stuff, like delivering great service, or building a long-term enduring brand will just happen naturally on its own."

–Tony Hsieh, interviewed at *Big Think*[5]

Culture Starts with Us: The Level 4 Leap

Tribal Leadership establishes five cultural levels at which an individual can react to a given culture. The first two, "life sucks" and "*my* life sucks," are hostile levels of resistance to successful and productive corporate cultures, the first one being plainly self-destructive and the second one more passive-aggressive. The book describes "leverage points" to help move people from

---
[5] http://bigthink.com/ideas/20672

the lower levels to a higher state, usually through socialization – networking with people in a higher tribal state who can act as mentors and even making friends on a higher cultural stage – and coaching – improving skills, responsibilities, and the perceived contribution to the group.

Level 1 and 2 cultures exist. Dilbert's office or Kafkian bureaucracies are a good example of level 2 cultures, where employees will feel victims of status quo, powerless to change it, complain about everything – which is always someone else's fault – and feel disconnected from the goals and vision of the company. Level 2 employees see the company as "a place to earn a living" and nothing else, and will try to goof off as much as possible.

It is in level 3 when we can start working our way to an Agile corporate culture. In level 3, the mantra changes to "I am the best (and you are not)." Level 3 is a quantum leap from levels 1 and 2, because here the person starts to realize his own power to perform and change things. Unfortunately, the problem with level 3 is that they fail at creating lasting structures in the form of teams, as level 3 cultures will set a continuous competition between members to see who's right. Winning, leading, ruling, and controlling are the goals of the level 3 person. They become arrogant and, as they are sure that their opinion is the only one that matters, they will try to get everyone to follow their criteria. Level 3 leaders can provide value, but their contribution will be gone with them as they will fail to set enduring structures that can work and perform on their own. Their personal goals will frequently be on top of those of the company, and they can't conceive that the organization can work without them holding the reins.

According to *Tribal Leadership* authors, an epiphany is needed for the level 3 person in order to understand that, to achieve a higher mean, he must collaborate with others in the search of a common tribe-wide objective. Level 4's mantra is "We are great – and they are not," as a typical characteristic of level 4 cultures is a common enemy, like Linux against Microsoft, Apple against Microsoft, Google against Microsoft, and, well, mostly everyone in the software industry against Microsoft.[6] Successful level 4 cultures, when given the opportunity to make history, will eventually move to level 5, "life is great," and achieve incredible results in the hyper-productive state, only to return to level 4 and wait for the next challenge at the end of the project or endeavor that allowed this transitory state.

---

[6] Just kidding, of course.

Of course, Agile and Lean cultures need a prevailing level 4 culture of teams, collaboration, systemic view, and empowerment. Lone riders, brilliant jerks, and personal agendas should simply not be tolerated, and the tribal leader should take care of them quickly and strongly.

Hiring and Firing According to Culture

When you study simple flow dynamics, or just when you apply some regular common sense, you learn that the content of a given system is the difference between what enters the system and what exits it. This simple law gives you three points where you must stress corporate culture: the people who enter your culture (hiring), the people who exit your culture (firing and turnover), and the people currently forming your culture (assessing, defining, communicating, reinforcing, and improving your current culture).

While most managers will already have an existing culture and maybe few opportunities to incorporate new hires or even fire people, some attention must be paid to the hiring/firing criteria and rules. All examples I have used to illustrate the concept of great corporate cultures (Google, Netflix, Zappos, Semco, *Good to Great*, *Tribal Leadership*) will stress the importance of hiring good matches for your culture and protecting your people from members of the tribe who go against the agreed values, noble cause, and way of working.

Regarding the hiring process, behavioral psychologist David McClelland concluded in his research on competence-based recruitment[7] that academic achievements of candidates are not totally related to future employee performance and value. His conclusion, after years of study, was that it is better to hire according to motivation, trait, values, and culture match and then train for knowledge and develop skills.

Netflix, for instance, looks for "the rare responsible person" on new hires: a mix of self-motivation, self-awareness, self-discipline, and self-improvement competencies. They look for people who will act as leaders and do what's needed, even if they are not told to do so. They often refer to people who "pick up the trash lying on the floor," as they feel like responsible people thrive on freedom and are worthy of that freedom. Having and honoring this kind of policy in every recruitment, using Rosing's words to describe Google's

---

[7] McClelland D (1973) Testing for competence rather than for intelligence. Am Psychol 28:1–14.

culture, "sets a cultural bit on people's heads – You are the boss. Don't wait to take the hill. Don't wait to be managed."

On the other hand, becoming a tribal leader means that you have to commit yourself to defend the half-espoused, half-emergent values, and noble cause of your corporate culture to the last consequences. That includes preserving the tribe if a member is acting against those values on a sustained basis.

Yes, Agile companies fire people. Sometimes we fail at identifying good matches for our culture – even Jesus had one Judas in his first 12 hires. When that happens, several approaches may be tested before firing:

- The conflictive person may be under-skilled and lack confidence. Training and developing that person may fulfill his need for competence and mastery.

- On the other hand, the conflictive person may need challenges that better suit his skill level. Assessing his true skills and adapting his assignments so they lie between boredom and anxiety – an exciting-enough challenge that can help the person learn but still be achievable – may motivate him to behave better.

- The trouble may be his current colleagues. Engaging the team and teaching them how to solve conflicts on their own may be a good start, but maybe trying this person in another team may provide a better match.

- The problem may even be a manager-employee issue. Trying him in a different department may be an answer.

Anyway, sometimes you just try all the tricks in the book and you still have a dysfunctional team member. I have a profound faith in people: I feel like everyone can be excellent at his job given the correct environment, culture, job, and guidance.

But sometimes I don't have enough resources to invest in someone, in the form of spending enough time with him or relieve him from his duties until he becomes a productive team member. Sometimes, on the other hand, I feel like re-gaining this person for the team is beyond my own coaching and managing skills. On those occasions, just looking away and hiring someone else to do his job will sooner or later backfire; as long as you have a clear policy of culture-matching hiring, this will be seen as incoherent behavior with established policies and culture, thus creating a culture of "one thing is what you can read on the posters and corporate guides, and then we have the *actual* things we do around here."

Another side effect of this behavior is to disqualify you as a tribal leader. When you fire someone for being contrary to corporate culture (after having tried several strategies), people will probably feel bad, as we are talking about a human being who was sitting with them and sharing coffee until yesterday – even if he was a pain in the back. Be prepared to explain to your people why you did so, why it is a good thing for the tribe as a whole, how this was coherent with tribal culture, values, and cause, and why this shall never happen to them.

As observed, they will feel bad for some time: some of them will understand later that this was probably in the best interest of the team and some will not. But on the other hand, if you just look away and let that person stay, then people will feel bad because they will see that matching the corporate culture and living its values is something optional – and of course you will have the current influence of that person and his behavior in corporate culture, which will sooner or later ruin it as a rotten apple ruins the whole basket.

The cost of firing someone is so high in terms of lost investment, low performance time before you fire him, damaged morale, and employee replacement cost, that the best advice I can give you here is to hire really, really slow. Many companies will complain that they need to hire very fast – this is, from my own perspective, a tremendous mistake – and others will claim that if they set new hire requirements too high, they will never find someone available. To all of them, I would really recommend to review Google's hiring process: it is known to be long, time consuming (as many as 16 interviews are conducted), and hard (they include several hands-on code tests and on-the-phone question answering), and, still, they've managed to hire 24,400 plus employees at a rate of several thousands a year.

Storytelling

So you need to have coherent policies on hiring and firing according to your corporate culture, but in order to have that, you first need to assess and define it. You also need to assess and define current culture and its future desired state in order to communicate it to the people who are currently on board. How can you do that?

Storytelling happens to be the best way to define and drive corporate culture. If you think about it, the best way to truly learn how things work in a given culture is not to read mission statements, annual reports, corporate strategy, or motivational posters but to hang out at the water fountain or coffee machine. There you will learn about the actual things that are happening, especially the ones that most impact people's morale and values. No one will possibly talk about filling reports, sending e-mails, or stamping forms – they are most likely to talk about an abusing boss, how they've spent the whole weekend coding, the post-retrospective party you ran past Friday, or how this client sent a personal message to your team giving them recognition for their great work and commitment.

If you review Netflix's or Zappos' corporate culture definitions, you'll realize how they use storytelling. Netflix lists their values and gives examples of what you do and don't, and even shows the case of employees questioning behaviors that are contrary to their culture. Zappos even asks its employees to write short stories about their culture and what they mean to them, and then compile them – unedited – in its corporate culture book.

Useful stories are those talking about people acting in a form that is coherent with their values. The contrary, stories about people acting incoherently to values, are only useful if the bad consequences of doing so are stressed – especially if those bad consequences don't come in the form of punishment, but direct causal effects of the incorrect behavior, so the importance of honoring these values is understood. Stories about people acting against values and nothing happening or nobody caring and acting accordingly will destruct your corporate culture project for sure!

Great stories are those that inspire people and give examples to follow. They connect to people's intrinsic motives both rationally and emotionally. Employees are more likely to be moved by stories of delighted customers or personal achievement than by ordinary-style company goals like "increasing market share" or "providing more value to stockholders." Stories are also easier to remember than a list of self-unrelated corporate values. Great stories can also serve as counter-stories: they can be used to rapidly react against gossip, rumors, and bad stories by providing counter examples, facts, and decreasing their impact.

> "To start a culture change all we need to do is two simple things:
> 1. Do dramatic story-worthy things that represent the culture we want to create. Then let other people tell stories about it.
> 2. Find other people who do story-worthy things that represent the culture we want to create. Then tell stories about them."
>
> –Peter Bregman, *Harvard Business Review*

Be careful: Corporate culture stories won't be found just in your company's most intimate circles. They will be everywhere. Clients will be talking about your products and services, and suppliers will tell stories about your payment process, your negotiation style, and your solvency and reliability. Competitors will be talking about your flaws. The press, social networks, stockholders, etc., pay attention to those stories too and use them to build your culture!

> "People don't believe what you tell them. They rarely believe what you show them. They often believe what their friends tell them. They always believe what they tell themselves. What leaders do: they give people stories they can tell themselves. Stories about the future and about change."
>
> —Seth Godin, *Tribes*

Change 101

So you want to change corporate culture?

Change is hard. Most managers are really concerned about the difficulties of fostering and driving change, and everyone who has ever tried to change a group of people, or even only one person's behavior, knows how frustrating it can be.

The truth is that you don't really "manage" change – although I'll still use the term "change management" – the same way you don't much "manage" a thunderstorm while sailing: all you can do is to hold on to the rudder and do your best to keep the boat floating. It doesn't matter if the storm pushes you hundreds of miles away from your course, for if you don't give up, the storm will be over sooner or later, and you will keep steering the boat to port.

Change is similar. It is a matter of a clear purpose and a strong commitment to stick to your guns, no matter how many times you fail in effecting change.

> "First they ignore you, then they laugh at you, then they fight you, then you win."
>
> —Mahatma Gandhi

But there is some good news too. All successful change processes seem to share a similar structure, and it has been thoroughly studied to produce a change-management body of knowledge.

The first thing you need to understand to successfully drive change is that our brain is hardwired to resist it most of the time. If the brain experiences a given situation for a long time, even an uncomfortable one, it will become the brain's own "comfort zone." Getting out of the comfort zone will be seen as a risky endeavor, as the new state will seem uncertain and the brain fears that which is not known. On the other hand, the delayed gratification of a possible better state can be overridden by the instant reward of doing nothing, meaning not having to face risks and invest energy.

All this reasoning is more emotional than really rational, but the rational brain will forge arguments to please the discomforted brain and help him stay in his comfort zone. In the end, changing anything means changing yourself, as your status, your role, your performance, and your comfort will change, and that is usually perceived by your brain as a threat.

> "Facing with the choice between changing one's mind and proving there's no need to do so, almost everyone gets busy on the proof."
>
> –John Kenneth Galbraith

So even if you are providing solid and rational arguments on the benefits of the change, be prepared to receive irrational resistance and don't frustrate yourself or take it personally: it's just the way our brains work by default.

The second fact to understand is that for every given group of people and every change proposed to the group, people will automatically fit into one of five arguing categories:

- *Innovators*, those proposing new ideas
- *Early adopters*, those adopting new ideas fast, even if they haven't been fully proven yet
- *Early majority*, the ones who will jump into the new idea as soon as it proves itself worthy and reliable
- *Late majority*, who will just do what everyone does
- *Laggards*, who will oppose anything and will try everything to remain the same

People can act differently depending on the group and the nature of change. Someone can be an innovator at work but a laggard at home, not wanting to change family traditions or habits. On the other hand, someone can be very innovative in technology but a laggard when it comes to social or organizational issues.

This division was first proposed by Everett Rogers, a professor of rural sociology, in his 1962 book *Diffusion of Innovations,*[8] and later on was popularized by Geoffrey A. Moore in his book *Crossing the Chasm,*[9] which discusses various strategies for successfully introducing new products to the market. In fact, both cases (diffusion of innovation and introducing new products) are just cases of change management, so the same model applies.

In both cases, the real challenge is to make the early majority use the product (or accept the change), as the early adopters will very surely accept it fast, the late majority will follow the early majority, and, no matter what you do, laggards will always complain. The "chasm" between early adopters and early majority is what change management tries to overcome.

The chasm-crossing process is based on two core action lines: finding the early adopters and maintaining the energy in the change process for enough time.

A Small Group of Brave Men

You must understand that making a change and driving change are not the same thing. When you want your environment to change, you should focus on communicating that vision to others and then let them actually *do* the change. If you focus on implementing the change by yourself or just command people to do it, you are using Tayloristic, hierarchical, level 3 tools – and you should start to read this book again from the beginning!

Finding your early adopters, and doing it in a subtle manner, is crucial. If you just address the whole group to propose an idea, you have big chances of laggards being the first to react: laggards shoot from the hip, and they will be fast in killing the initiative. The idea of making an inspiring speech and convincing everyone so they break into tears, stand on their tables, and yell

---

[8] Everett M R (1962) Diffusion of innovations. The Free Press.

[9] Moore G (1991) Crossing the chasm: marketing and selling high-tech products to mainstream customers. Harper Business Essentials.

"Oh captain! My captain!," no matter how beautiful it sounds in your mind, is not very likely to happen.

On the other hand, a small group of early adopters is all you need to start your change process. Think of it this way: it is not that a small group of people can't really change anything – it is more that every significant change that you can find in human history, from Christianism to freedom from slavery, was started by a small group of committed and relentless men.

Creating a first community of peers who share your interest and constantly nurturing that community is the best way of achieving significant changes. In some way, what you are doing is planting the seeds of future change while you collect your first evidence and experience to, later on, convince the early majority.

The early majority will demand some track. They will want to see a group of people already implementing the change. They want success, excitement, pilot trials, etc. They want stories! Storytelling is also a crucial part of change management. Stories that demonstrate change, create a vision, and ignite action are a good way to move a passive majority to join a change effort.

As for corporate culture change, what you are probably doing is building tribes from scratch and that means leading and connecting people with similar ideas.

> "What we do for a living now, all of us I think, is find something worth changing and then assemble tribes that spread the idea so it becomes something far bigger than ourselves – it becomes a movement.
>
> So when Al Gore set out to change the world again, he didn't do it by himself and he didn't do it by buying a lot of ads – he did it by creating a movement: thousands of people around the country who could give his presentation for him, because he can't be on 500 of cities each night."
>
> –Seth Godin, "Tribes" Ted Talk[10]

Addressing early majority members is useful: they will often be rationally skeptical about the change, and their arguments can give you clues and

---

[10] Available at www.ted.com/talks/seth_godin_on_the_tribes_we_lead.html

feedback about the main leverage points you should be using to make them cross the chasm. Some members of the early majority can be opinion leaders, and if you discuss their concerns with them and make them join your community of early adopters, you'll start moving other members of the early and late majority. But remember not to spend time arguing with laggards, as they will just be change-adverse and usually have a low opinion leadership.

Taking Your Time

Overnight change is a myth. The problem is that people only realize change when it happens on a massive scale. Everyone notices the snow avalanche, but no one seems to be watching the whole process since the first snowflakes start to accumulate.

Consider, for example, Angry Birds, the gaming phenomenon. Lots of people considered it to be an overnight success, but the truth is that small game developing company Rovio had made 50 previous products you'd probably never heard about.

Another example: Don Dodge, Google's former business development director and now developer advocate, calls the "Guitar Hero" franchise "a 10-year overnight success"[11]: it was the ninth video game produced by Harmonix, 10 years after founding the company. For the previous 9 years, Harmonix tried to create new ways to teach music to nonmusicians, and their idea never really took off.

What is the lesson here? As my good friend and start-up rock-star Alejandro Barrera usually says, "keep pushing!" Even the slightest daily push, if maintained daily during enough time, will have a compound-interest effect. Jim Collins, in *Good to Great*, calls this the "Flywheel Effect": starting to move the flywheel until it has its own momentum.

Compare the flywheel effect to usual "change programs," where a crisis is detected and urgent change is imposed on everyone – like a top manager opening his corner-office door and shouting "go change!" to everyone, banging the door closed an instant later. Constant reinforcement of the change process is needed, as well as providing constant energy to the

---

[11] http://dondodge.typepad.com/the_next_big_thing/2011/10/how-early-product-failures-led-to-huge-successes.html

system, which otherwise will start to rapidly deteriorate and revert to the pre-change state. The problem, as Mark Fields noticed while driving change at Ford, is that "Culture Eats Strategy for Breakfast," so for sustaining a change strategy, you have to constantly "keep pushing."

> "I have been observing lean transformations for longer than I'd care to admit and I have come to terms with the feeling that you're always failing with what you are doing right now—even though you might be succeeding over all. At least 50% of the time I visit the Gemba to observe people working on 5 S, red bins or pull systems (just to name a few), I get dispirited: the 5 S has gone to the dogs and needs to be restarted, or the red bins are no longer being treated with the respect they deserve, or the pull system is down again. And so on. This, I have painfully come to accept, is normal. We're not constructing a building. We're training a team. A team of people, which means that we will have ups and downs, none of which means that we aren't making progress. Especially when we keep in mind the main thing: what we are really doing here is beefing up our firms problem-solving capability. Short-term stumbles are fine as long as we are clear on our long-term goal."
>
> –Michael Ballé, Lean Enterprise Institute

Sustained momentum can't be built upon isolated non-followed-up trainings, monthly meetings, periodical events, regular reports, or specific goals. In case you wonder, I have my own recipe for building momentum and driving change:

- *Courage*: a fearless approach. Change agents will often be afraid of judgment, failure, or loss of status if the change fails.

- *Commitment*: devoting enough energy, time, and resources to personally keep the change process going.

- *Discipline*: maintaining the effort over time, never losing focus.

- *Proactivity*: overall, you can't just tell people to change. You have to walk the talk, inspire others, and be the first to represent the change you want.

> "You must become the change you want to see in the world."
>
> –Mahatma Gandhi

Change Patterns

Apart from nurturing a community of change agents and dedicating time to it, there are several change patterns that you can use to energize the change process and take it to the early majority.

In their book *Fearless Change: Patterns for Introducing New Ideas* (Manna and Rising 2004), Mary Lynn Manns and Linda Rising list a set of change patterns they've identified through numerous change experiences in a variety of sizes and types of organizations throughout the world. The interesting concept behind change patterns is that they've been systematically identified in several cases, proving their usefulness in different situations. Patterns are named and described in the book in a way that will help you understand how to use them.

Through the use of those patterns, you can design your own change strategy by selecting the ones more suitable to your own, specific situation. For instance, if you are beginning your change process, you can start by "asking for help" (not trying to do it alone), find "innovators" (people who are quick to adopt new ideas), "plant the seeds" (carry materials, or seed, that you can "plant" in places where people will pick them), and play the role of an "evangelist" (to introduce a new idea into your organization, let your passion for this new idea drive you). On the other hand, if you are far into the change process, you may want to "involve everyone" (make it known that everyone is welcome to be part of the change effort and try to involve people from as many different groups as possible), remind people "in your space" (placing reminders of the change idea around your organization where people are likely to see it), or have a "guru on your side" (enlist the support of experienced, senior-level gurus who are respected by both managers and non-managers alike).

"Fearless Change" patterns will also give you a language and a framework to study other change initiatives and understand their positive effects, thus making it easier to learn about them and use their lessons in your own change endeavor.

Summary

No matter how good your motivation, self-organization, structuring, and workload Agile management strategies are, if they are not correctly aligned with corporate culture, you are most likely to fail in your Agile adoption plan. On the other hand, the right culture will automatically drive people into the Agile path. The right culture can be enforced with a combination of "level 5" leaders, the right people on board, and a strong discipline and commitment to meet the cultural vision.

Cultures are defined in terms of common values and a noble cause. There must be a strong alignment between espoused values, those communicated through management and formal structures, and assumptions, the underlying actual beliefs, behaviors, and values of the people who form the organization. The right set of values should be enforced through hiring and firing, as well as constantly reminding the people in the company through the use of storytelling.

If an Agile culture is to be set, teamwork and a "we are great" mantra should be observed over individual-aimed, competitive-based goals. Lone riders can be great as novelists, actors, or even freelancers, but there is little place for them in a level 4 Agile culture.

Changing the corporate culture is a big challenge. A clear purpose must be stated, and the set of innovators and early adopters should be identified and enrolled in a long-term project. "Level 5" leaders should then commit to a proactive and constant change effort, where courage and strong discipline will be needed. A set of change patterns have been observed that can help the change agent keep the fire lighted.

Things to Try

- Find the "First Follower: leadership lessons from a dancing guy" video online. Serious. You'll learn a lot on how change happens and how nurturing your early adopters and sustaining the change process long enough will help you succeed with your change initiative.

- If you didn't look at Netflix presentation on corporate values when we discussed motivation and autonomy, do it now. Even if you already looked at it, review it again under the perspective of a corporate culture – goals, a noble cause, and storytelling.

- Go to www.zapposinsights.com, learn more on Zappos culture, and ask for their free culture book online.

- Assess your prevalent tribal stage. As you will learn if you read *Tribal Leadership*," tribal stage can be observed in the language people use, for example, the use of "I am/I do" instead of "we are/we do." Depending on your prevalent stage, find leverage points to move people to the level 4 epiphany. Be sure to understand your current culture before trying to change it!

- Start building your own corporate culture presentation or book – look first at Netflix's presentation or Zappos' book. Start a storytelling culture at your company. Inspire people to give examples of good behaviors and identify common values, then gather them together and communicate them frequently. Actively engage discussions on these stories and how they can help you achieve your common goals.

- As proposed in Chap. 4, find and communicate a noble cause for your company, group, department, or team.

- Remember that artifacts also affect and nurture a corporate culture. Set your people free to make their environment match their culture.

- Incorporate cultural match rules in your hiring process. You can also research Google's hiring process and policies and read Joel Spolsky's *Guerrilla Guide to Interviewing.*[12] Joel is a software engineer, writer, founder of Fog Creek Software, and a thought leader in the software community. His interviewing guide can give you some insights on how to reengineer your hiring process.

- Find a company whose culture you admire and try to connect to someone there. In the Internet age, this is easy to achieve using professional tools and social networks like LinkedIn or even Facebook or Twitter. Ask them for advice and try to learn more on how that company sustains corporate culture. People with great corporate cultures are eager to talk about them!

- Download and study Fearless Change patterns. They are available at http://www.fearlesschangepatterns.com

- Play the "miracle game" with your people. Imagine that a miracle happened this weekend and changed the company culture to the desired state. Then ask your people to describe how they would notice the change on Monday morning – focus on those leverage points to start your change process.

---

[12] http://www.joelonsoftware.com/articles/GuerrillaInterviewing3.html

Recommended Readings

Collins J (2001) Good to great: why some companies make the leap. . .And others don't. HarperBusiness, New York

Collins J, Porras JI (1994) Built to last: successful habits of visionary companies. HarperBusiness, New York

Denning S (2005) The leader's guide to storytelling: mastering the art and discipline of business narrative. Jossey-Bass, San Francisco

Godin S (2008) Tribes: we need you to lead us. Portfolio Hardcover, New York

Heat C, Heath D (2010) Switch: how to change things when change is hard. Crown Business, New York

Hsieh T (2010) Delivering happiness: a path to profits, passion and purpose. Business Plus, New York

Logan D, King J, Fischer-Wright H (2008) Tribal leadership: leveraging natural groups to build a thriving organization. Harper Business, New York

Manns ML, Rising L (2004) Fearless change: patterns for introducing new ideas. Addison-Wesley Educational Publishers Inc, London

Moore G (1991) Crossing the chasm: marketing and selling high-tech products to mainstream customers. Harper Business Essentials, New York

Final Thoughts

Positive and Useful Insights for the Agile Walk

9

Continuous Improvement and the *J*-Curve

The *J*-curve is a frequent behavior map where results first fall for a while but then rise higher than the starting point. When you invest your money in something, your bank account's balance will drop – the money is not there anymore – but when you hopefully start receiving revenues from your investment, it will slowly rise to the point that you'll end up having more money that you had before.

The same way, when you add people to a software development team, performance will first drop because of Brooks' law, but as soon as the new members start to learn and effectively integrate into the team, they will start to increase the team's performance. When team performance beats its previous state, they will start to reduce the "delivery debt" created while training the newcomers, and they will reach a point where all the invested time will be delivered back and the team's capacity will be higher from there on.

The *J*-curve, sometimes called the investment cycle, is a life-guiding principle for me. It is a way to illustrate Lean's "long-term thinking" that should guide the Agile manager as well. When you invest time on motivation, self-organization, learning, improving, nurturing the culture or cross-training team members, the first effect will inevitably be a drop in performance: if you panic and stop the effort, you will be failing in one of the two main components of the change process – maintaining the effort through time.

Be sure to always spare enough resources to invest in the long term, even at the cost of short-term losses.

Á. Medinilla, *Agile Management*, DOI 10.1007/978-3-642-28909-5_9,
© Springer-Verlag Berlin Heidelberg 2012

Baseball Does Not Work

There is a great article by XP cofounder Ron Jeffries titled "We Tried Baseball and It Didn't Work." Go read it. Now.[1]

The article is a brilliant allegory of what happens when you try to introduce an idea, Agile in this case, but start clipping out all the parts that seem wrong, uncomfortable, not suitable for your organization, or just too hard to try. Then you end up with something comfortable that doesn't work, and you blame Agile.

I really feel like all the ideas in this book, as much as they come from many different sources, are strongly interconnected. Start cherry-picking the set and you'll inevitably break it. Imagine what will happen if you take one of the small rule sets discussed in the chapter about self-organization, like the one birds use to flock or the ants to find food, and remove some of the rules.

Take Agile as a whole and consider it as a whole. If you find it appealing and believe it is the best thing for your company, go for the whole.

Agile Is Not a Place

There is no "Agile" state. Agile is not a place nor is it a binary condition where you are Agile or you are not (despite the opinion of many Agile zealots who love to label things as "not Agile"). Even the Agile Manifesto, the only authoritative source of what's Agile and what's not, has a principle saying that "Continuous attention to technical excellence and good design *enhances agility*." So it seems like Agility is something that can grow and decrease.

In fact, Agile is an endless path. A search for an ideal, utopian state of perfection that we most probably will never reach, but still guides us through continuous improvement and a perpetual sense of discomfort to an always better state: today, better than yesterday. Tomorrow, better than today.

During the journey... enjoy the path! The path is the whole point of Agile. Instead of thinking of Agile as something to earn or reach, better depict it as taking a first step in a given direction, and then keep on walking indefinitely.

---

[1] http://xprogramming.com/articles/jatbaseball/

Remember also how the ant was able to eat the elephant: taking a small bite every day.

What Message Are You Communicating?

This is a good question to ask yourself before you do anything as a manager. Suppose that it is your birthday and someone bought you a fancy espresso coffee machine. You decide to place it in your own office. What message are you communicating to the people drinking the goo that comes out of the canteen's coffee machine? Now think that you place your fancy new espresso coffee machine where everyone can use it. Different message, right?

Everything a manager does sends a message. A whole team I was coaching some time ago was paralyzed for weeks only because, while they were meeting with some other teams, the manager entered the room, took a look at everyone, and said "gee, what a whole bunch of people," and then left the room.

For the manager, who was actually looking for some quiet place to work, it was an innocent comment, but the team understood that they had been scolded for goofing off or something worse. The mistake, here, was that the team's Agile coach didn't raise the team concerns to management immediately – they only found out 2 weeks later when I had a follow-up meeting with the team.

You have to remember that even if you don't see them, all managers carry invisible six-guns on their hips.

Masakatsu Agatsu

Aikido founder Morihei Ueshiba was a famous martial artist, often referred to as "Ōsensei" ("Great Teacher") by all other Japanese martial artists. He was one of the most important martial artists of all times, an influential philosopher, and received Japan's Order of the Sacred Treasure in 1968.

He coined the expression "*Masakatsu Agatsu*," which can be translated as "true victory is victory over oneself." This, again, is a life-guiding principle for me. It is also relevant for the Agile manager, for if you are calm and maintain control over yourself, you will be able to reframe your managerial state and stop conceiving it as a continuous and frustrating fight with those who resist your will.

The Agile manager must develop himself before he is able to develop others. This development must cover all aspects of his life, including empathy, self-growth, personal relationships, self-control, and general balance.

Overall, an Agile manager must gain absolute control of his own ego. Ego will drag you to level 3, Tayloristic, arrogant behavior, and fill you with anger and frustration when you face resistance. Furthermore, ego won't let you trust and rely on others, so you will not be able to effectively lead them in an Agile way.

Remember that in the Agile world, it is not about you anymore: it is about us.

Index

Á. Medinilla, *Agile Management*, DOI 10.1007/978-3-642-28909-5,
© Springer-Verlag Berlin Heidelberg 2012

Printed by Publishers' Graphics LLC